HIGH above
EGYPT

THE AMERICAN UNIVERSITY IN CAIRO PRESS

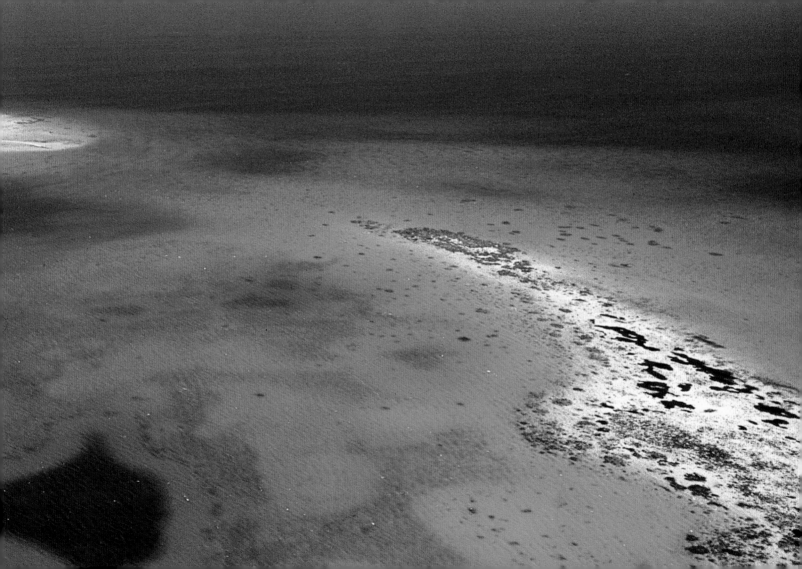

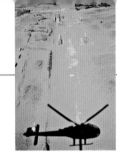

HIGH ABOVE EGYPT

PHOTOGRAPHS AND INTRODUCTION

Marcello Bertinetti

FOREWORD

Omar Sharif

TEXT

Corinna Rossi

graphic design
PAOLA PIACCO

graphic realization
PAOLA PIACCO
PATRIZIA BALOCCO LOVISETTI

translation
CATHERINE BOLTON

First published in Egypt in 2004 by
The American University in Cairo Press
113 Sharia Kasr el Aini, Cairo, Egypt
www.aucpress.com

Third printing 2009

Dar el Kutub No. 8829/04
ISBN: 978 977 424 873 3

© 2004 White Star S.p.A.

Color separation by Fotomec, Turin
Printed in China

1
The Pyramids of Khafra and Khufu.

2-3
The Temple of Karnak, composed
of three sacred precincts.

4-5
The White Desert.

Contents

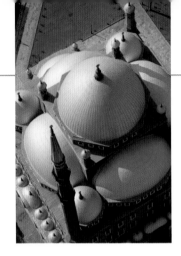

6-7
The Nile Delta near the city of Damietta.

8-9
The coral reef of the Strait of Tiran in the Red Sea.

10
The Temple at Tebtynis.

11
The Gordon Reef in the Red Sea.

12
The mosque of Mohammed Ali in Cairo.

13
The First Pylon of the Temple of Luxor.

14-15
Aloft in a hot air balloon over Luxor.

Foreword

by Omar Sharif

EVERY TIME I RETURN TO EGYPT, AS THE PLANE SEEMS TO FLOAT
GENTLY DOWN TOWARDS ITS FINAL DESTINATION, THERE IS A MO-
MENT AS I GAZE OUT OF THE WINDOW WHEN IT FEELS AS THOUGH I
AM SITTING ON A FLYING CARPET, SUSPENDED MAGICALLY ABOVE
CAIRO, LOOKING DOWN ON THE MOTHER OF THE WORLD BELOW ME.
THE GRACEFUL MINARETS AND DOMES, THE JIGSAW OF FLAT-
ROOFED BUILDINGS, THE VARYING PATTERNS OF THE STREETS, EVEN
THE TINY CARS MOVING SLOWLY LIKE BEETLES ON THE SAND—FOR
AN INSTANT I AM LOST ONCE MORE IN ASTONISHMENT AT THE BEAU-
TY OF A WORLD SEEN FROM ABOVE, AND NOT JUST ANY WORLD, BUT
CAIRO, A UNIVERSE IN ITSELF. AND THEN I THINK: WHAT WOULD IT BE
LIKE TO FLOAT LIKE THIS OVER THE WHOLE OF EGYPT? TO SEE ITS
GREAT RIVER, ITS FIELDS, ITS DESERTS, ITS VILLAGES, ITS MOUNTAINS,
AND ITS MONUMENTS FROM THIS EXTRAORDINARY VANTAGE POINT?

TO LOOK DOWN ON FELUCCAS ON THE NILE, PALM GROVES IN THE OASES, CORAL REEFS UNDER THE WARM WATER OF THE RED SEA, PYRAMIDS AND TEMPLES IN THE SANDS? TO FEEL THE SILENCE AND TRANQUILITY OF A PATCHWORK WORLD, FAR BELOW BUT CLOSE ENOUGH TO TOUCH?

NOW THIS BEAUTIFUL BOOK HAS TAKEN ME ON JUST SUCH A MAGICAL RIDE, WITH MANY SUCH UNFORGETTABLE MOMENTS—AND I DON'T WANT TO COME DOWN.

The
author

MARCELLO BERTINETTI, WAS BORN IN VERCELLI, ITALY, IN 1952. HE WAS A NATIONAL AND INTERNATIONAL EPÉE CHAMPION, COMPETING AT THE 1976 OLYMPICS IN MONTREAL AS A MEMBER OF THE ITALIAN TEAM. AFTER GRADUATING WITH A DEGREE IN MECHANICAL ENGINEERING, HE DEVELOPED A PASSIONATE INTEREST IN PHOTOGRAPHY, BECOMING A FREELANCE PHOTOGRAPHER IN 1978. SINCE THEN, HE HAS COLLABORATED WITH MANY PRESTIGIOUS INTERNATIONAL MAGAZINES AND PUBLISHERS, WORKING ON NEWS REPORTS AND SUCCESSFUL PHOTOGRAPHY BOOKS, AND HANDLING ADVERTISING MEDIA. IN 1984 HE AND VALERIA MANFERTO DE FABIANIS FOUNDED THE PUBLISHING FIRM OF WHITE STAR. BERTINETTI HAS COMBINED HIS WORK AS A PUBLISHER WITH HIS CAREER AS A PHOTOGRAPHER.

Introduction

by Marcello Bertinetti

IT IS COLD AND DARK AT LUXOR, BUT THE STARRY SKY PORTENDS AN EXTRAORDINARY MORNING. THERE'S NO WIND, AND THE SILENCE WEAVES A MAGICAL ATMOSPHERE. I LOOK AT MY FRIEND MARK LINZ AND MY INTERPRETER GAMAL SHAFIK, WHO IS ACCOMPANYING US. THEY LOOK BACK AT ME, AND THEY TOO ARE QUIET. MAYBE WE'VE FINALLY DONE IT. IT FEEL AS IF A LIFELONG DREAM IS ABOUT TO COME TRUE, BUT I CAN'T ENJOY IT YET, OUT OF FEAR THAT SOMETHING, OR SOMEONE, WILL BREAK THIS SPELL. THE PILOT OF A POWERFUL RUSSIAN MI-17 HELICOPTER CALLS OVER TO US: WE CAN LEAVE BEFORE DAWN! I NERVOUSLY CHECK THE CAMERAS STRUNG AROUND MY NECK. EVERYTHING IS READY. SOMEONE STRAPS THE SAFETY BELTS ON ME

21

In this stunning panorama, the city of Luxor is illuminated
by the morning sunlight.

AND I REMAIN SEATED ON THE FLOOR OF THE HELICOPTER, MY LEGS SWINGING IN THE AIR THROUGH THE OPENING: I HAD THE HATCH REMOVED TO MAKE IT EASIER FOR ME TO TAKE PICTURES.

WE'RE OFF, AND THE THRILL IS INSTANTLY UNBELIEVABLE.

THE SUN ISN'T UP YET, BUT IT IS ALREADY GETTING LIGHT. THE GRAY PENUMBRA SHROUDS THE TEMPLE OF KARNAK, CREATING A SURREAL AURA AND GIVING IT A SENSE OF TIMELESSNESS. PEOPLE ARE STILL ASLEEP, AND THE LANDSCAPE BENEATH US SEEMS CRYSTALLIZED IN AN UNNATURAL IMMOBILITY.

THE IMAGE OF KARNAK, WITH THE RIBBON OF THE NILE AND THE DESERT MOUNTAINS IN THE BACKGROUND MARKING THE CONFINES OF THE VALLEY OF THE KINGS, HAS BEEN CAPTURED BY THE FILM IN MY CAMERA. BUT ABOVE ALL, IT IS ETCHED IN MY MIND. I CONCENTRATE ON THESE IMAGINES, BUT I FEEL AS IF I HAVE STEPPED OUT OF TIME AND AM RELIVING THE PAST. I TAKE IN ITS ATMOSPHERE AND LET MYSELF BE LULLED BY ITS RHYTHM.

WE COME TO DEIR AL-BAHARI, AND I REALIZE THAT THE SUN IS

STARTING TO RISE. I TURN AROUND TO SEE THE DAWN OF A NEW ETER-
NAL MORNING IN THEBES.

I SWING BACK AROUND AND AM STUNNED: THE DESERT HILLS
AROUND THE TEMPLE OF HATSHEPSUT ARE AWASH IN AN IMPOSSIBLE
SHADE OF RED. IT IS A FANTASTIC SIGHT AND THERE I AM, IN THE RIGHT
PLACE AT THE RIGHT MOMENT, ON AN ORDINARY DAY OUT OF TIME.

I CONTINUE TO FOCUS ON THESE IMAGES. I FEEL CALM BUT DECISIVE,
AND WITHOUT THE LEAST HESITATION I SNAP PICTURES WITH DIFFER-
ENT F-STOPS. WE CIRCLE AGAIN AND THE VALLEY OF THE KINGS APPEARS
BEFORE ME, INCREDIBLY COLORFUL AND SPLENDID WITH ALL ITS
TREASURES. THERE IS NOT A SINGLE PERSON IN SIGHT.

WE CIRCLE YET AGAIN. I'M READY TO TAKE MORE PICTURES, BUT
THE LIGHT HAS ALREADY CHANGED, TURNING ORANGE AND QUICKLY
FADING TO YELLOW. IN A MATTER OF MINUTES, A MIRACLE HAS HAP-
PENED—AND THEN VANISHED—BUT NOW THE ROLLS OF FILM ARE IN
THE POCKET OF MY JEANS, AND I FEEL INCREDIBLY LUCKY.

I FINALLY DID IT, BUT IT TOOK ALMOST EVERY OUNCE OF PATIENCE

TO GET THERE, TO EXPERIENCE AND CHERISH THOSE FATEFUL THREE MINUTES.

OVER THE COURSE OF THREE YEARS, I SPENT MORE THAN 60 HOURS AIRBORNE OVER EGYPT, WITH THE EGYPTIAN ARMY AND IN A HOT AIR BALLOON, AND I TOOK ABOUT 20,000 SLIDES.

I FLEW OVER THE MEDITERRANEAN COAST BETWEEN MARSA MA-TRUH AND THE SUEZ CANAL, WHERE THE DAZZLING WHITE SAND DUNES MEET THE BLUE WAVES.

I CARESSED ALEXANDRIA—A BREATHTAKING CITY—AND AS YOU LOOK DOWN ON IT FROM THE SKY YOU CAN STILL IMAGINE THE PRES-ENCE OF ITS LEGENDARY LIGHTHOUSE.

IN THE NILE DELTA I SAW FISHERMEN WITH THEIR BOATS, AND A MYRIAD OF CULTIVATED FIELDS THE COLOR OF EMERALDS.

THE NILE: ITS NAME ALONE IS ENOUGH TO MAKE ANYONE TREMBLE WITH AMAZEMENT, CURIOSITY, AND ADMIRATION. POWERFULLY, IT FLOWS: THE BEARER OF LIFE, THE SYMBOL OF EGYPT AND ITS GREAT CIVILIZATION.

I FLEW OVER CAIRO, AN INFINITE METROPOLIS WHOSE TENTACLES

HAVE NOW REACHED THAT MIRACLE OF ENGINEERING KNOWN AS THE PYRAMIDS. ENORMOUS, THEY STAND SILENTLY PROUD IN THEIR PERFECT FORM, PROTECTED BY THE DISQUIETING PRESENCE OF THE SPHINX—A HUMAN FACE AND FELINE BODY—THAT HAS LOST NONE OF ITS POWERFUL MYSTERY OVER THE CENTURIES.

IN THE GREAT WESTERN DESERT I SAW PALE SAND DUNES CARVED BY THE WIND. I SAW THE ROCKS AND MOUNTAINS OF THE WHITE DESERT, WHICH LOOK AS IF THEY ARE COVERED WITH SNOW, EVOKING AN ANCIENT MIRACLE. AND THEN THERE ARE THE OASES, EXQUISITE EMERALDS SET IN THE SAND: SIWA, THE LEGENDARY DESTINATION OF ALEXANDER THE GREAT AND KNOWN FOR ITS SPLENDID LAKES, BAHARIYA, FARAFRA, AND FAYUM.

AT LUXOR I RELIVED THE TRUE ATMOSPHERE OF ANCIENT EGYPT, IN SEEMINGLY ENDLESS ECSTASY. THE TEMPLE AT LUXOR, THE TEMPLE AT KARNAK… THEY ARE INCREDIBLY PERFECT. FROM ALOFT, YOU CAN PERCEIVE HOW THEY WERE ONCE CONNECTED TO EACH OTHER BY A LONG AVENUE OF SPHINXES, BY LAND, AND BY THE NILE.

I CAN PICTURE THE FESTIVAL OF OPET, WHEN THE PHARAOH, IN HIS BOAT WITH HIS RETINUES, TRAVELED MAJESTICALLY DOWN THE NILE BETWEEN THE TWO TEMPLES.

TO THE WEST ALONG THE NILE, THE HILLS CONCEAL THE VALLEY OF THE KINGS AND THE VALLEY OF THE QUEENS, WITH THE GREAT TEMPLE OF MADINET HABU, THE RAMESSEUM, THE TEMPLE OF SETI I AND THE COLOSSI OF MEMNON STANDING OUT NEXT TO THEM.

AMIDST THESE IMPRESSIVE RUINS, FARMERS LIVE JUST AS THEY DID THOUSANDS OF YEARS AGO, THEIR DAYS MARKED BY THE MOVE-MENT OF THE SUN. FROM ABOVE, I TOOK IN THIS ANCIENT SPECTACLE AND PHOTOGRAPHED IT IN ALL ITS EVOCATIVE GLORY.

FOLLOWING THE GREEN BANKS OF THE NILE, I ARRIVED AT ASWAN, WHERE THE RIVER OPENS UP INTO CATARACTS TO CREATE A PLACE OF RARE BEAUTY. WHITE FELUCCAS GLIDE SILENTLY ALONG THE SAPPHIRE RIVER, PAINTING A VIVID IMAGE AGAINST THE PALE SAND.

BUT IT IS LAKE NASSER THAT, VIEWED FROM ABOVE, STIRS MY DREAMS. ITS AZURE WATERS AND EXPANSE IN THE DESERT WEAVE A

SURREAL VISION. SANDY STRIPS JUT INTO IT LIKE FINGERS, YET THE LAKE HOLDS FAST AND, INDEED, STRIKES BACK, PERHAPS EVEN GAINING NEW TERRAIN. THE TEMPLES ON ITS SHORES ARE SENTINELS, THE IM-MUTABLE WITNESSES OF A BATTLE WAGED IN SILENCE AND SOLITUDE.

THE TEMPLE OF WADI AL-SEBUA HAS ITS OWN ALLURE, AND IT IS THE PRELUDE TO MAJESTIC ABU SIMBEL, THE IMMENSE MONUMENT TO RAMESSES II AND HIS ROYAL WIFE NEFERTARI. FROM ABOVE, THE GREAT TEMPLE VIRTUALLY SEEMS TO DOMINATE THE ENTIRE DESERT, THE LAKE, ALL OF EGYPT AND BEYOND.

THE LANDSCAPE AND ATMOSPHERE CHANGE DRAMATICALLY WHEN YOU REACH THE SHORES OF THE RED SEA. THE CORAL REEFS FLAUNT BRILLIANT COLORS, CREATING A VERITABLE LIGHT SHOW IN THE CRYSTALLINE WATERS.

DESERT ISLANDS SEEM TO BREAK AWAY FROM THE COASTLINE, LIKE JEWELS LOST IN A BLUE EXPANSE. TINY WAVES RIPPLE THE SUR-FACE OF THE SEA, AND THE SALT AIR MAKES IT CLEAR TO ME THAT EVERYTHING HERE IS DIFFERENT. OFF IN THE DISTANCE, I SEE RAS MO-

29
Ras Mohammed, completely barren of all vegetation, juts from
the southernmost tip of the Sinai Peninsula.

HAMMED, THE SOUTHERNMOST TIP OF THE SINAI PENINSULA,

STRETCHING INTO THE RED SEA. THIS IS WHERE I USED TO GO DIVING

MORE THAN THIRTY YEARS AGO WITH MY LIFELONG FRIENDS CARLO,

GIANNI, AND SERGIO: THIS IS WHERE I WOULD COME FOR ADVENTURE.

I CAN'T HELP BUT GAZE DOWN AT THIS SCENE WITH A SENSE OF AF-

FECTION, AND A TOUCH OF SADNESS: IT IS MAJESTIC AND BEAUTIFUL.

FOR ME, EGYPT IS FAR MORE THAN A MERE DESTINATION. IT IS PART

OF MY VERY SOUL, AND EACH ONE OF MY PHOTOGRAPHS REVEALS

MY FEELINGS AND MY MARVELOUS MEMORIES.

30-31
The white sands and crystal sea in front of Marsa Matruh
create countless nuances of blue.

32-33
The Great Sand Sea "flows" near the Farafra Oasis.

34-35
The Great Sphinx of Giza.

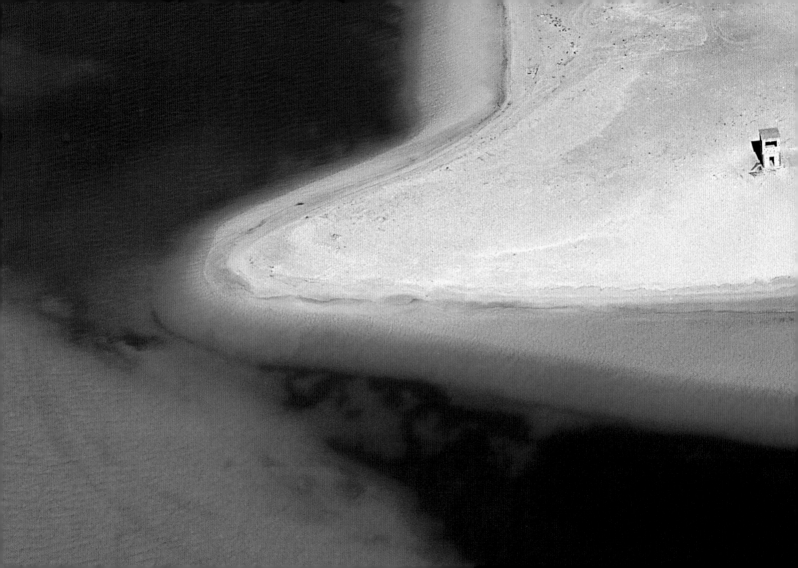

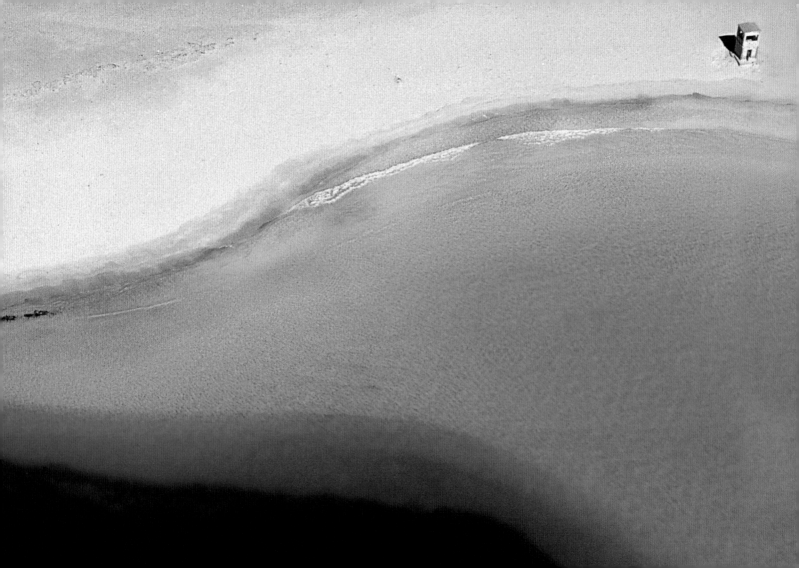

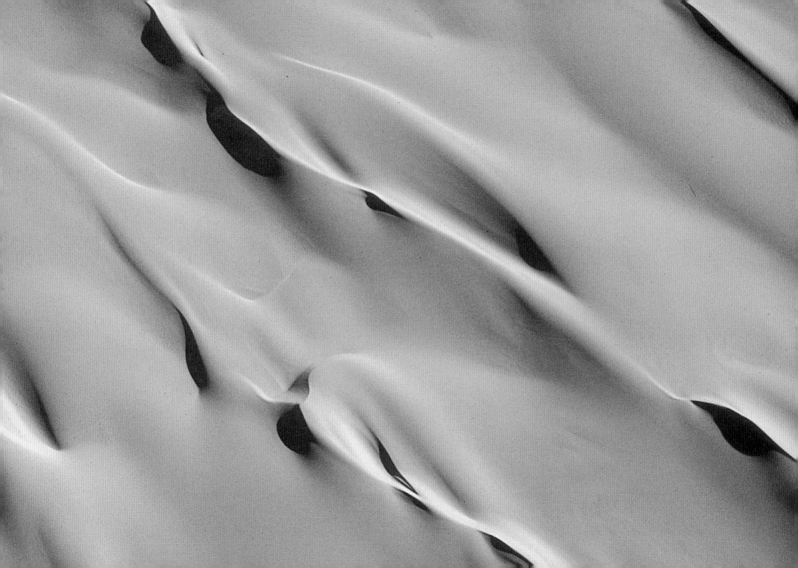

IN THE KINGDOM OF THE PHARAOHS

HIGH ABOVE EGYPT

37
The Giza pyramids (left) and the Hypostyle Hall of the
temple at Karnak (right).

The history of Egypt under the pharaohs spans thirty centuries. The invention of writing, which marks the transition from prehistory to history, took place in about 3000 B.C., shortly before the legendary pharaoh Menes united the two kingdoms of Upper and Lower Egypt under his rule. The three thousand years that followed have conventionally been divided into the Old, Middle, and New Kingdoms, followed respectively by the First, Second, and Third Intermediate Periods, times of weak or contested rule; they are followed by the Late Period and the Greco-Roman Period. The sequence of pharaohs who ruled Egypt has been divided into thirty dynasties, based on the reconstruction drawn up by the priest Manetho, who lived in the third century B.C. Nevertheless, these classifications, although useful tools of reference, must not be interpreted too rigidly. For example, the centralized state had every reason to paint the periods in which the central authority was weak or crushed as disastrous, but this does not necessarily mean that the so-called Intermediate Periods were marked by obscurantism and destruction. Likewise, at times it is unclear why the succession from one pharaoh to another should mark a dynastic change. In any event, the powerful dynasties that ruled during stable periods did indeed leave extraordinary monuments that to this day bear witness to the sophistication and genius of the ancient Egyptian culture. The archaeological remains of Egypt under the pharaohs extend along the banks of the Nile for over

38
Subjected to restoration work since antiquity, even today the exterior of the Great Sphinx of Giza is constantly monitored and repaired as needed.

In the kingdom of the pharaohs

900 kilometers, and they are also present in the Delta, the Sinai Peninsula, and the deserts. The country's ancient division into two states, Upper and Lower Egypt, stems from the substantial difference that exists even today between the course of the Nile, a narrow and symmetrical landscape, and the Delta, a vast and lush area crisscrossed by numerous canals, and once covered in part by swamps. The third key region in Egyptian history—and whose import is somewhat underestimated—is the desert. Graffiti and rock carvings found along the wadis of the Eastern Desert and on isolated boulders in the heart of the Western Desert demonstrate that their mineral resources quickly attracted the attention of the Egyptians. The Sinai Peninsula also enjoyed a golden age, as demonstrated by the evocative temple of Serabit al-Khadim, part constructed and part sculpted in rock. There is no question that the Delta, with its wealth of flora and fauna, was inhabited from most ancient times. Because of its fertility and geographical position near the Mediterranean and the

Middle East, the region gradually became so important that Ramesses II, the best known pharaoh of the Nineteenth Dynasty, built a vast residence there for himself and for his court. The Delta's most famous city is Alexandria, which was founded by Alexander the Great (died 331 B.C.) on his return from Siwa, and under the Ptolemies (323–30 B.C.) the city became one of the Mediterranean's most important centers of Hellenistic culture. The famous library, which was later destroyed by fire during the first century B.C., was the backdrop to the mathematical studies of Euclid and Archimedes, and the astronomical discoveries of Apollonius and Ptolemy.

The last part of the Nile Valley, just before the river divides to form the Delta, has an astonishing concentration of archaeological remains from the period of the pharaohs. The area has thus been the destination for generations of travelers and scholars, past and present. The symbols of Egypt recognized the world over—the immense pyramids at Giza built by Khufu, Khafra, and Menkaura—stand out against the

In the kingdom of the pharaohs

desert background, dwarfing all else around them: the vast ancient necropolis, the village of the workers who built them, and even the tentacles of the great city of Cairo that now reach them.

As we move south, the desert skirting the line of the Nile Valley to the west is dotted by a sequence of funerary complexes with dozens of pyramids, large and small, and hundreds of tombs of the pharaohs' subjects. First we come to Abusir, where the pharaohs of the Fifth Dynasty built their monuments, and then to Saqqara, an important necropolis throughout the Old Kingdom. This is where the pharaoh Djoser built the very first pyramid, in the shape of a sequence of steps of decreasing size. Nearby are the inconspicuous remains of Memphis, the ancient capital of the Old Kingdom that is now buried under cultivated fields and modern towns. A little farther south at Dashur are the pyramids built by Khufu's father Snefru, including the Bent Pyramid, the first one designed as a smooth pyramid from the very outset. The sequence continues with the pyra-mids of the Middle Kingdom, once as spectacular as those of the Old Kingdom but now reduced to irregular piles of rubble. Moving upstream, among the remains of settlements and burial grounds from various eras, we come to Amarna, the city founded during the Eighteenth Dynasty by the pharaoh Akhenaten to shift power away from Thebes, capital during the New Kingdom, and make room for a new religion centered on worship of the solar disk. Unlike Amarna, which was forgotten after Akhenaten's time, Abydos has a millenary history: the burial place of the pharaohs of the earliest dynasties and the location of an important temple, its necropolis extends for kilometers and includes a notable series of cenotaphs built by the pharaohs of the Middle and New Kingdoms. The area of ancient Thebes, the capital of Egypt during various periods of history, is filled with archaeological remains. In fact, together with Cairo it is one of the country's most important tourist destinations. The east bank of the Nile was occupied by the great complexes of Luxor and Karnak. The latter was composed of three

43
The Pyramid of Khafra at Giza is one of the few that still has part of its original cladding. The pyramids were generally finished in prized limestone.

44-45
The pyramids at Giza were built on the hard, rocky surface of a plateau that rises from the sands of the surrounding desert.

temples dedicated to Amun, Mut, and Montu, which were connected by wide paths lined with statues of sphinxes and rams. Concealed by the peaks rising on the west bank are the Valley of the Kings and the Valley of the Queens, where the pharaohs of the New Kingdom were buried in rich tombs built by a community of workers and artists who lived in the village of Deir al-Medina, up in the mountains. At the foot of the slope toward the Nile, the most powerful pharaohs also erected great temples to celebrate their cult: Hatshepsut built Deir al-Bahari; Seti I, the temple of Qurna; Ramsses II, the Ramesseum; and Ramesses III, Medinet Habu. The Colossi of Memnon are all that remain of the temple of Amenhotep III. The remains of a series of great temples built during the Greco-Roman Period are located in Upper Egypt: Dendera and Edfu, dedicated to the goddess Hathor and the god Horus respectively, and Kom Ombo, a peculiar double temple dedicated to two deities, Sobek and Haroeris, and lastly the complex of temples on the island of Philae, south of Aswan, which were disassembled and then reconstructed on a neighboring island after the Aswan High Dam was completed in 1970. Before Lake Nasser was created, the course of the river was interrupted here by the first of six cataracts, which created a natural barrier of great strategic importance. The Egyptians occupied the island of Elephantine in ancient times and during certain periods they successfully controlled the territory of Nubia, now submerged by the lake. After the High Dam was constructed, several monuments such as the temples of Abu Simbel, constructed by Ramesses II, were saved through the massive work of disassembling and reconstructing them at sites beyond the reach of the lake. Others, such as the chain of fortresses built by the warlike pharaohs of the Twelfth Dynasty to conquer and control Nubia, were submerged forever.

The Giza plateau

46

Like the Pyramid of Khufu, that of Menkaura (in foreground) at Giza was accompanied by three smaller pyramids for three queens.

47

The pyramids at Giza were surrounded by a vast necropolis, which included hundreds of tombs of the nobility and the royal family.

In the kingdom of the pharaohs

48-49
Cairo has developed along the road that connects the pyramids to the Nile. Once a tree-lined avenue crossing cultivated fields, today this road is a highly trafficked thoroughfare.

50 and 51
During the day, the pointed shadow of the pyramids slowly crosses the surface of the plateau. At a certain point, the shadow of the Pyramid of Khafra strikes the base of the Pyramid of Khufu and the museum housing the Solar Boat.

52 and 53
The sides of the Pyramid of Khafra are 15 meters shorter than those of the Pyramid of Khufu, and the height is 3 meters lower. However, since it is almost 1.5° steeper, it looks taller. The reduced size and increased inclination helped save on the volume of stone used to build the monument, but without detracting from its grandeur.

54

The continuous line of the cladding of the upper part of the Pyramid of Khafra gives us an idea of the original appearance of all Egyptian pyramids.

55

Unlike the Pyramids of Khufu and Khafra, the lower part of the Pyramid of Menkaura was clad in granite.

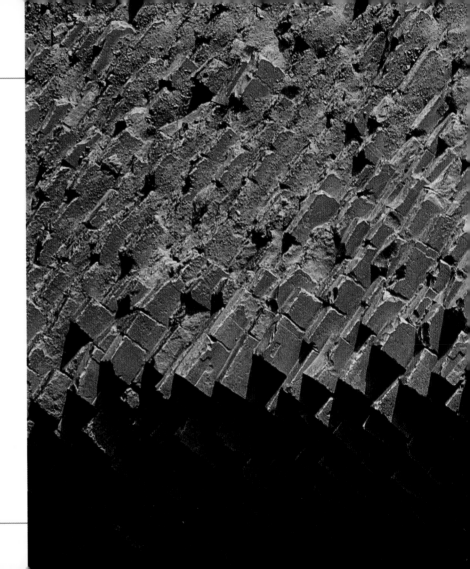

56-57
The height of the small portion missing at the top of the Pyramid of Khufu is replicated by a wooden structure.

58 and 59

In addition to building an enormous pyramid for himself, Khufu also constructed three pyramids for his queens and built at least five housings for large wooden boats. These boats may have been used to exploit the flooding of the river and carry the pharaoh's body to his tomb.

60
The Sphinx lies between the ancient ceremonial causeway of the funerary complex of Khafra and the modern
road leading to the top of the plateau.

HIGH ABOVE EGYPT

62 and 63

Khafra constructed a temple for himself, visible at the end of the ceremonial causeway, and one for the Sphinx, set across from it.

64-65

Approximately 20 meters high and 73 meters long, the Sphinx was the first colossal statue in the history of ancient Egypt.

66

The granite stele set between the paws of the Sphinx dates from the reign of Tuthmosis IV, and it bears witness to the restoration work done on the oldest statue known today.

67

The Sphinx wears a *nemes* on its head. This piece of fabric wrapped across the forehead and widened at the sides of the head, decorated with a snake in the middle, was the headdress typically worn by the pharaohs.

68 and 69
The funerary temple of the Pyramid of Sahura was built using different stones: granite for the base, limestone for the wall, and basalt for the floor. The funerary temple of Sahura contained bas-reliefs depicting the pharaoh in hunting and war scenes.

Abusir

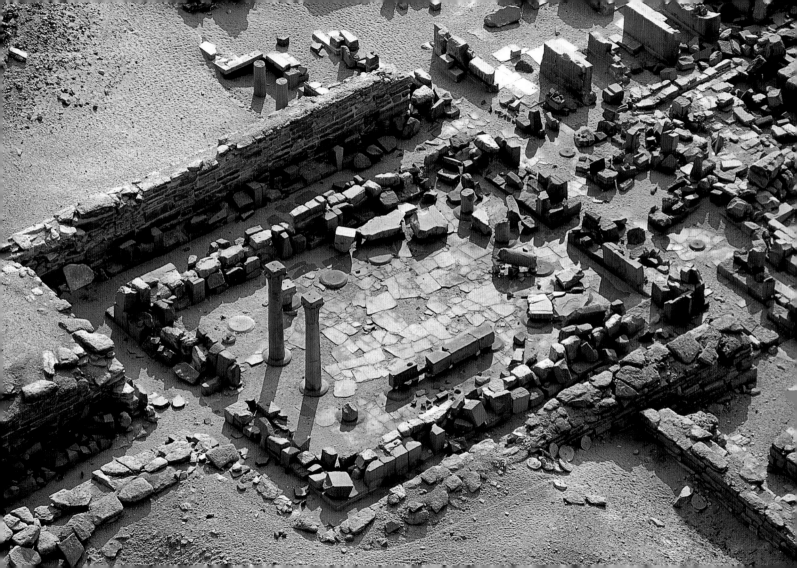

70 and 71
Like the other pharaohs of the
4th Dynasty, Pepi II chose
Saqqara as his burial site, building his pyramid here. Next to it is
a funerary temple with a ceremonial ramp connecting it to a
valley temple.

Saqqara

Saqqara is a large necropolis that was used since the most ancient times. Its most important monument is the funerary complex of Djoser with its famous step pyramid.

74

The step pyramid of Djoser, which covered a funerary apartment composed of dozens of underground corridors, is the oldest stone construction of ancient Egypt.

75

Next to his pyramid at Saqqara, Pepi I built at least five pyramids for his queens; each pyramid had its own small mortuary temple.

76-77
Part of the ramp of the pharaoh Unas, located next to the enclosure built by Djoser, was constructed using blocks from the latter.

78-79
The funerary complex of Djoser at Saqqara was surrounded by a continuous wall that had only one entrance.

80-81
Enormous chapels delineate the Heb-sed court, where the great king Djoser was crowned.

82 left
At Saqqara, the tombs of the New Kingdom are quite different from the ancient mastabas and pyramids. In effect, they are more like miniature temples than tombs.

82 right
Four immense piers rise at the exit of the colonnade that led to the main courtyard of the complex of Djoser, across from the pyramid.

83
For the jubilee celebration, the king had to complete a ritual race. These horseshoe elements inside the funerary complex probably marked one of the ends of the route.

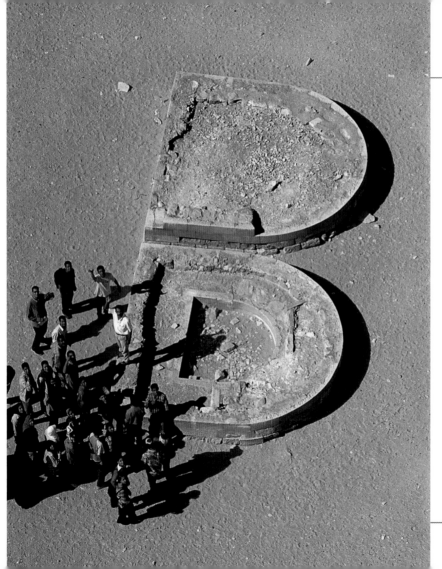

Saqqara

84

Many of the buildings around the step pyramid have no interior space and essentially play only a symbolic role.

85 left

Two rows of ritual buildings face the courtyard named for the *heb-sed*, the pharaoh's jubilee.

85 right

The North and South Pavilions were built alongside the step pyramid; both pavilions had a small open courtyard.

87

The Bent Pyramid—also known as the Rhomboid Pyramid—
owes its name to the sharp change in the slope of the monument, decided by the architects halfway through its construction.

Dahshur

88 and 89
After Djoser, at least three other pharaohs built themselves step pyramids like the one at Saqqara. At the beginning of the 4th Dynasty, the Bent Pyramid was the first to be built from the outset as a "smooth" or "geometric" pyramid.

90 and 91
Unlike the finishes on nearly all other pyramids, much of the cladding of the Bent Pyramid has survived. Only the lower part and the corners of the monument have been damaged by time and by human activity.

Dahshur

92 and 93
When the Bent Pyramid was nearly finished, Snefru started building another pyramid near the first one. This monument is known as the Red Pyramid due to the reddish stone used to build it.

HIGH ABOVE EGYPT

95
The top of the Red Pyramid. The burial chamber within is reached by means of a descending corridor and via two almost identical antechambers.

96
The Bent Pyramid was completed by a small funerary temple
(bottom left) and was surrounded by an enclosure with a small
satellite pyramid next to it (top left).

HIGH ABOVE EGYPT

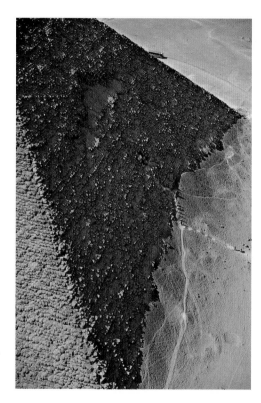

98 and 99

The entrance to the Red Pyramid, which can barely be distinguished at the top of zigzag steps, is on the north side. This is the traditional position for the pyramids of the Old Kingdom.

Memphis

100 and 101

Today, little remains of Memphis, the capital of ancient Egypt for centuries. Several colossal statues and groups of architectural fragments give us an idea of the grandeur of the monuments that once stood in the area.

102
Seven centuries after Snefru, Amenemhat III built his "Black Pyramid" in sight of the Bent Pyramid and the Red Pyramid.

103
Removal of the stone cladding exposed the core structure of the Black Pyramid, made of mud bricks, which has partly disintegrated.

Meidum

104-105
The Pyramid of Meidum was built by Huni, the last pharaoh of the 3rd Dynasty and the father of Snefru.

In the
kingdom
of the
pharaohs

106 and 107
The Pyramid of Meidum, originally a step pyramid, was modified twice. Another step was added for a total of eight, and then the monument was transformed from a step pyramid into one with smooth faces, which eventually collapsed.

108

When the exterior stone cladding was removed from the pyramid built by Senwosret II at Lahun, all that was left was a mass of mud bricks.

110-111

From left: the Giza pyramids; the top of the Pyramid of Khafra; the Sphinx; the Pyramid of Djoser; the Pyramid of Meidum; the so-called Bent Pyramid.

Lahun

Fayum

112 and 113

The original nucleus of the small temple of Medinet Madi, located at the edge of the cultivated fields of the Fayum Oasis, was built during the Middle Kingdom and then repaired during the New Kingdom. During the Greco-Roman Period, the temple was extended on both the front and back, and it was decorated with statues of crouching lions.

114 and 115
Thanks to its agricultural production, during the Ptolemaic Period the Fayum Oasis became one of the richest regions in Egypt. Like other towns and villages in the region, Tebtynis flourished.

116 and 117

Two stone statues portraying crouching lions mark the access to the small Ptolemaic temple at Tebtynis, flanked by buildings made of mud bricks.

118-119
The remains of the city and of the great temple of Dimai, connected by a long ceremonial causeway, date back to the Greco-Roman Period.

121
Like the complex of Karnak, the Temple of Luxor was expanded a number of times over the centuries by all the most important pharaohs.

Luxor

In the kingdom of the pharaohs

122
At Luxor, massive roofless architraves rest over the colonnade of Amenhotep III, composed of two rows of seven supports rising to a height of nearly 16 meters.

123
The Temple of Luxor is accessed through the pylon built by Ramesses II. There were originally two obelisks in front of it.

124 and 125

The history of the Temple of Luxor extends well beyond the era of the pharaohs. During the fourth century AD the temple was converted into a Roman fortress, Subsequently, numerous Christian churches were built inside it and, lastly, during the thirteenth century the mosque of Abu al-Haggag was built over part of the court of Ramesses II, where it is still located today.

126
The great complex of Karnak was built on the east bank of the Nile, and its entrance was originally accessed from the river.

Karnak

128 and 129
A vast field of ruins marks the places once occupied by the different enclo-sures of the temple complex of Karnak. The most impressive remains are those of the great Temple of Amun, the main subject in these two photo-graphs.

HIGH ABOVE EGYPT

131
The first courtyard of the Temple of Amun at Karnak was crossed by a giant colonnade built by the pharaoh Taharqa of the 25th Dynasty.

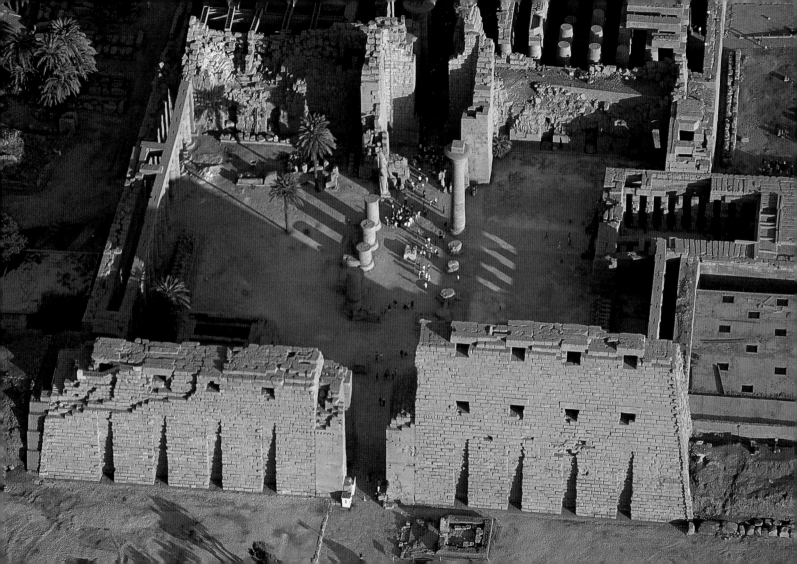

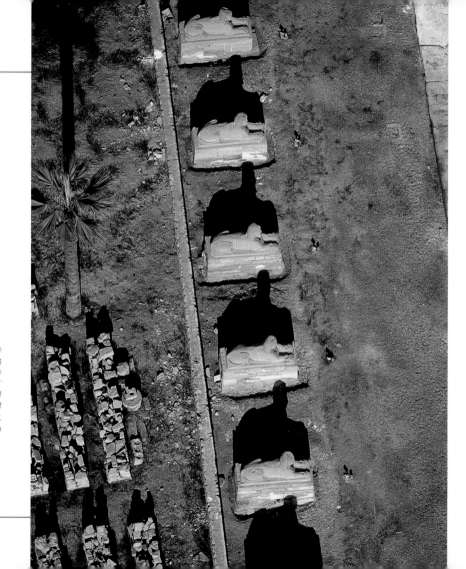

132 and 133
A systems of avenues lined with stone statues representing rams, sphinxes with human heads and sphinxes with rams' heads, linked the enclosure of Amun at Karnak to the wall of Mut and the Temple of Luxor, which was located more than a kilometer to the south.

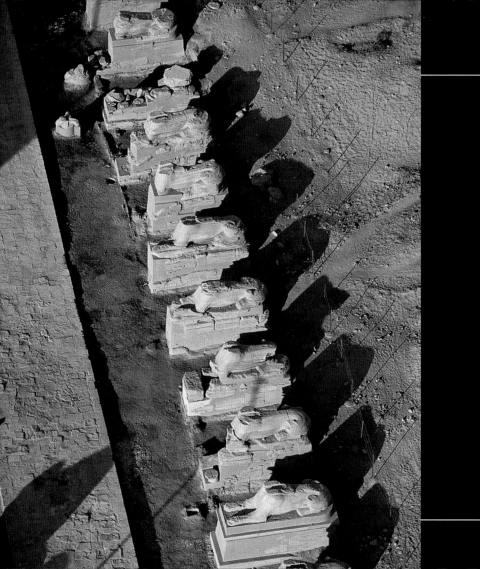

HIGH ABOVE EGYPT

134 and 135

The impressive Hypostyle Hall of the Temple of Amun at Karnak, built by Amenhotep III, was composed of two side colonnades covered with massive architraves and a taller central corridor. Light filtered into this central part through tall windows.

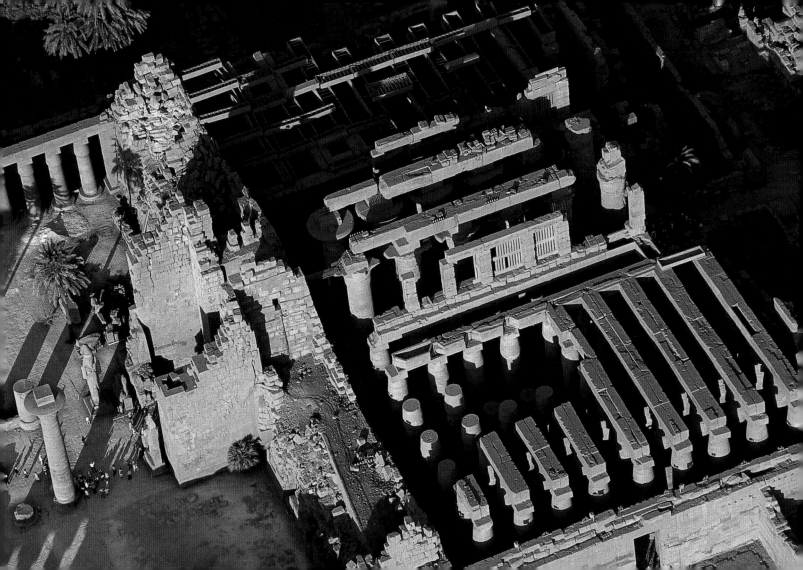

HIGH ABOVE EGYPT

137
A large rectangular sacred lake occupies the space between the oldest section of the Temple of Amun at Karnak and the series of pylons on the south side.

138
Another irregularly shaped sacred lake surrounds the remains of the Temple of Mut inside the southern enclosure of the complex at Karnak.

140-141
The eighth pylon of the Temple of Amun at Karnak was built by Tuthmosis III and was decorated with colossal statues.

West
Thebes

142

The light of dawn illuminates the two pylons and the chapel of the mortuary temple of Ramesses III, at Medinet Habu, enclosed by the ruins of the mud-brick wall that enclosed the area.

143

The west bank of the Nile across from Luxor is dotted with a series of mortuary temples, including Medinet Habu, built by Ramesses III.

Medinet
Habu

144-145
The bas-reliefs on the entrance
pylon at the temple at Medinet
Habu portray Ramesses III as he
crushed Egypt's enemies.

In the kingdom of the pharaohs

146-147
Since it was surrounded by thick walls and had a large complex of secondary buildings, Medinet Habu quickly developed into a fortified city.

148-149
The bases of enormous columns rise amidst the ruins of the Hypostyle Hall of the Temple of Medinet Habu. To the left and right, different rooms housed chapels and mortuary annexes.

Deir al-Bahari

150-151
A tall ridge, crossed by paths cleared in ancient times, encircles the temples at Deir al-Bahari and conceals the Valley of the Kings.

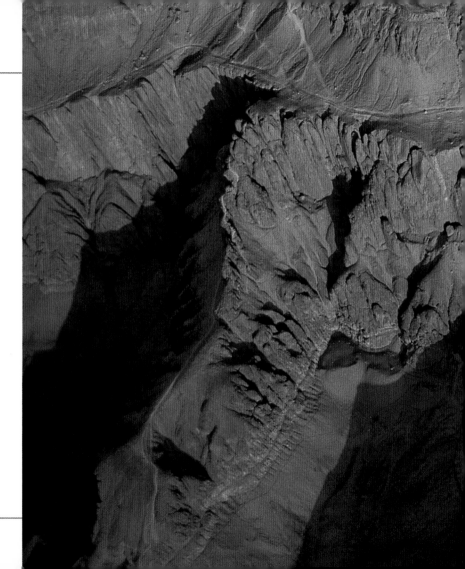

152 and 153
The spectacular natural basin of Deir al-Bahari was chosen by Mentuhotep, the first pharaoh of the 11th Dynasty, to build his innovative mortuary temple. More than five centuries later, Queen Hatshepsut exploited the same dramatic backdrop and built her large temple, with a series of terraces, alongside the first temple.

154
Wide paths and low walls have been built at the Valley of the Kings to facilitate tours of the site and mark the entrances to the tombs.

155
Parts of the Temple of Hatshepsut at Deir al-Bahari underwent extensive restoration work by the archaeologists who studied the monument

Royal tombs

156 and 157
Minuscule rectangular shadows dot the floor of the Valley of the Queens (left) and that of the Valley of the Kings (right). They mark the entrances to the underground tombs, cutting many meters deep into the rock face.

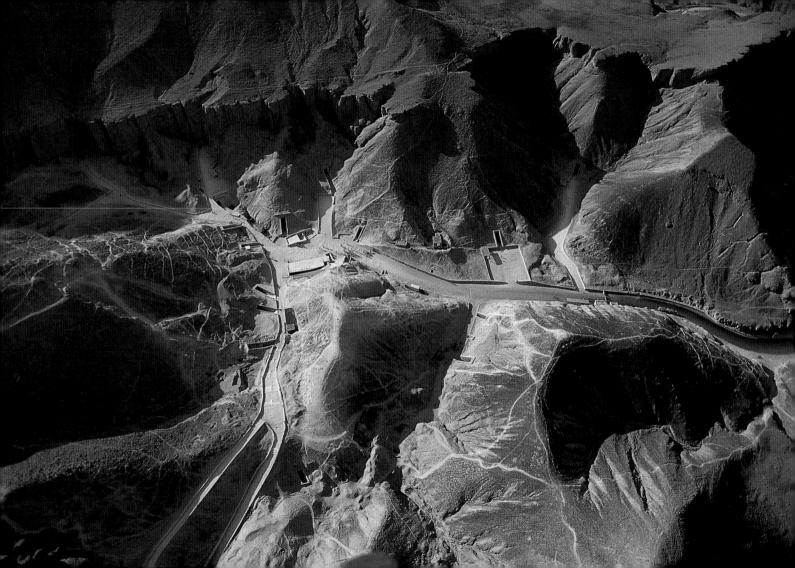

158
The ancient Egyptians named the mountain dominating the
Valley of the Kings *Meret-seger*, which means "She who loves
silence."

HIGH ABOVE EGYPT

161

Ramesses II had a vast mortuary temple built for himself on the west bank of Luxor. Today, the monument is referred to simply as the Ramesseum.

The Ramesseum

162 and 163
The great walls of the Ramesseum enclosed a temple built in stone, of which the ruins of the vast hypostyle hall remain, as well as a large number of storerooms made of mud bricks and arranged in rows along three sides of the temple.

164
Stone slabs cover the hypostyle hall of the Ramesseum.

165
Colossal statues of Osiris and of the pharaoh decorated the open courtyard that led to the hypostyle hall.

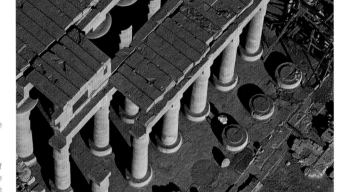

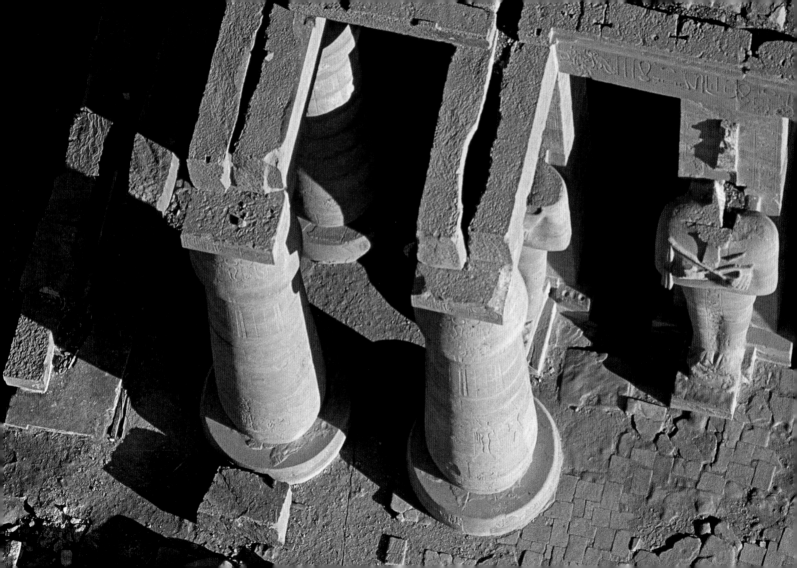

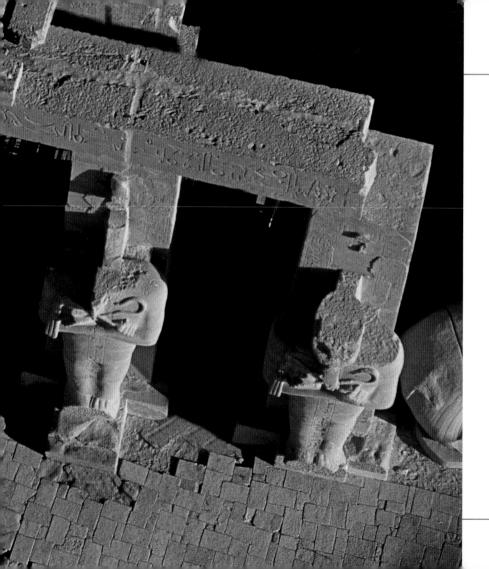

166-167
In the courtyard of the Ramesseum, the Osiris pillars of Ramesses II were subjected to the iconoclastic rage of the early Christians who settled around Thebes.

Deir al-Medina

168
The workers who built and decorated the tombs in the Valley of the Kings and Valley of the Queens lived in the village of Deir al-Medina, not far from the royal necropolis.

169
The shadow of a balloon can be seen on the small Ptolemaic temple built of stone near the village of Deir al-Medina.

170 and 171
The Ptolemaic temple at Deir al-Medina was built in a sacred area that already held the remains of older temples, which were constructed during the New Kingdom.

172-173
The village of Deir al-Medina was surrounded by walls inside which narrow roads led to the workers' dwellings.

175
Seti I built his large mortuary temple, which also included a
small royal palace, on the plains across from the entrance to
the Valley of the Kings.

Al-Qurna

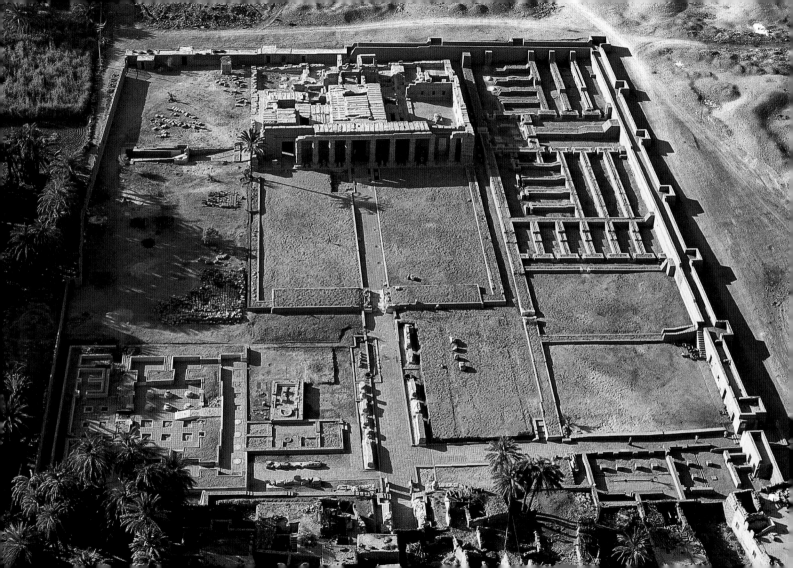

The
Colossi
of
Memnon

176 and 177
The Colossi of Memnon once stood in front of a pylon at the sides of the east entrance to the Temple of Amenhotep III.

178-179
Only two colossal statues remain to bear witness to the ancient presence of the enormous mortuary temple of Amenhotep III.

Dendera

Edfu

182 and 183
The Temple of Horus at Edfu is now surrounded by the modern city of Edfu and by mounds of mud bricks, all that remains of the old city.

Kom Ombo

184 and 185

The Ptolemaic temple at Kom Ombo was devoted to two gods, Sobek and Haroeris. As a result, it was built with two entrances on two parallel axes that ended with a pair of sanctuaries set side by side at the back of the temple.

Philae

189
After the Aswan Dam was built, the small Graeco-Roman temple of Dakka was moved more than 40 kilometers north of its original position.

Nubia

190 and 191
Chased by the shadow of the helicopter, a caravan of drome-daries transits in front of the Temple of Wadi al-Sebua, built by Ramesses II in arid Nubia, at the southern end of the king-dom.

192
The small Roman temple of Maharraqa is unique not only in its design but also in the presence of a spiral staircase leading to the roof.

193
The interior of the small temple of Dakka, which had two sanctuaries, is covered with well-preserved inscriptions and decorations.

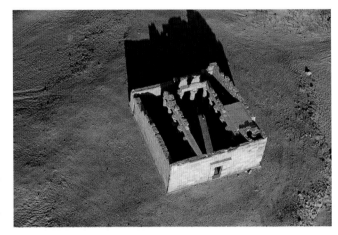

Abu Simbel

194 and 195

The main temple of Abu Simbel is flanked by four colossal statues that are over 20 meters tall and were carved into the face of the mountain.

196-197

The temples of Abu Simbel, the work of Ramesses II, are among the most famous monuments of ancient Egypt. In order to be moved after the Aswan Dam was built, they had to be dismantled into blocks and an artificial hill was created for them.

THE DESERTS
THE SANDS OF KEMET

HIGH ABOVE EGYPT

HIGH ABOVE EGYPT

199
Enormous dunes near Lake Nasser (left); the arid mountain
chain near Deir al-Bahari (right).

The Nile Valley, with its colors, vegetation, cities, villages, noise, people, and vehicles, occupies only a small part of Egypt. Along the riverbanks, the vegetation grows thick and luxuriant as far as the water can reach, but then it abruptly turns to desert. Beyond this clear line of demarcation, space expands and silence reigns.

As you cross the desert, you realize just how varied it is. First of all, there are the colors. The lower half of the panorama you see before you displays every possible shade of yellow, brown, and gray, often with rich touches of pink and purple. The upper half is taken up entirely by the blue of the sky, which is sometimes reflected in the hot sand, creating mirages of tantalizing pools of water. The landscapes can also differ enormously. The rocky peaks of Sinai and the Eastern Desert seem to chase each other, going from the brown of the nearest peaks to the purple of those in the distance, and they are framed by the deep blue of the sea often visible in the background. In the Western or Libyan Desert, we encounter limestone formations like those of the famous White Desert of Farafra, as well as sweeping plateaus shot through with crystal veins or dotted with dark globular boulders.

A closer look reveals that even the sand dunes are highly diverse, depending on the terrain and the direction of the wind. Seif or "sword" dunes form long sharp ridges and always move in

200
A layer of sand, its surface carved by the wind, runs across
the limestone floor of the desert near the Farafra Oasis.

The deserts: the sands of Kemet

the same direction; crescent dunes—known also as barchans—fluctuate but generally move according to the prevailing winds; and star dunes spin around on themselves in groups, yet always remain in the same spot.

Dunes moving in any given direction can be small enough to devastate a bush in their path, or large enough to swallow up rocky hills, roads, and villages, the battered remains of which subsequently reemerge years later from behind the dunes. Nothing can stand in the way of sand dunes: they scale plateaus, descend into valleys, and even climb on top of one another, creating enormous dappled masses of sand. The dunes also reproduce, generating miniature replicas from their extremities. These new dunes then develop rapidly and go their own way.

The central part of the desert bordering Libya is covered by the Great Sand Sea, an expanse of dunes set one after the other as far as the eye can see, stretching for hundreds of kilometers. In-

deed, viewed from above, it resembles a yellow sea of motionless waves. And somewhere in that expanse lie the buried remains of Cambyses' army. According to legend, 50,000 men were sent by the Persian king in 524 B.C. to the Oasis of Siwa to destroy the Oracle of Ammon. Greek historian Herodotus related that "the armies sent against the Ammonians departed from Thebes accompanied by guides; it appears that they arrived as far as the Oasis.... What happened then can be recounted only by the Ammonians or by those who heard it from them, and no one else; because [the troops] did not reach the Ammonians, nor did they return.... They were nearly halfway there ... when a great southerly wind swept down on them as they were intent on eating, a wind so impetuous that it buried them all under immense piles of sand. Thus, an entire army disappeared."

It is this constant movement of sand—sometimes slow and imperceptible, sometimes sting-

The desert: the sands of Kemet

ing with the fury of the wind—that shapes the desert. Here, we find only soft lines, smoothed corners, eroded surfaces. Traces vanish quickly on the sand, and each irregularity in the surface tends to be connected to the rest by a continuous line. If you walk on a rippled surface, it can be difficult to interpret its contours, but if the same area is viewed from the air, everything suddenly becomes clear. In areas dotted with archaeological remains, the even lines of ancient buried buildings, the borders of fields cultivated thousands of years ago, and surfaces riddled with forgotten cemeteries magically appear, as though a veil had been lifted.

Both now and in the past, aerial views have played an important role in interpreting the territory. Exploration of the heart of the Libyan Desert, which began toward the end of the nineteenth century, started to move at a faster pace in the 1920s and 1930s when a number of intrepid Egyptian and foreign explorers made vital contributions

that filled in the enormous gaps on the maps of the era. Prince Kamal al-Din was the first to map the Gilf Kebir, the vast plateau that covers the southwest corner of Egyptian territory. The Gilf held out against the vehicles of explorers for years, and its final conquest did not occur until Count Laszlo Almásy and Sir Robert Clayton led an airborne expedition in 1932 that explored the territory from the sky. The Aqaba Pass was identified the following year, and even today it allows motor vehicles—unable to cross the area until then—to reach the top of the plateau.

The history of desert exploration and of the exploitation of its resources dates back centuries. The intricate network of the wadis of the Eastern Desert played an important role during the time of the pharaohs in connecting the Nile Valley to the shores of the Red Sea.

When the Romans took control of Egypt, they adopted this road network, even improving on it by building a series of fortified cisterns and wells.

Small villages on west bank at Luxor nestle at the foot of the mountain, which is crisscrossed by trails that date back thousands of years. The Valley of the Kings is hidden behind the mountain.

Likewise, the immense rocky and sandy stretches of the Western Desert are crisscrossed by ancient caravan routes. Today, some of these routes have been replaced by paved roads, but others have survived as trails, marked by the passage of the travelers who used them over the centuries. Old pottery shards and camel bones have now been joined by empty gas tanks, burst tires, glass bottles, and tools left on the sand by impromptu mechanics while repairing a vehicle.

Crossing the Libyan Desert has never been easy. In the second half of the fourth century A.D., Athanasius of Alexandria wrote that the oases of the Western Desert were where "one goes to die if he has been fortunate enough to reach them alive, and if he has not already died along the desert trails to reach them."

Nevertheless, the desert has an appeal that goes beyond exploration for scientific or geographical purposes. Exploring the desert can, on a more spiritual level, mean eternal and boundless seeking, a quest for the unknown and for infinitude. Indeed, it is telling that the symbols representing exploration of the Libyan Desert, past and present, have remained the same: the Gilf Kebir, Cambyses' lost army, and the elusive oasis of Zerzura.

As Ralph Bagnold wrote in *Libyan Sands* in 1934, "I like to think of Zerzura in that light, as an idea for which we have no apt word in English, meaning something waiting to be discovered in some out-of-the-way place, difficult of access, if one is enterprising enough to go out and look; an indefinite thing, taking different shapes in the minds of different individuals according to their interests and wishes.... Zerzura is sought in many places, in the desert, at the Poles, in the still unsurveyed mountain regions of Asia.

"There is no fear that the quest will end, even though the blank spaces on the map get smaller and smaller.... As long as any part of the world remains uninhabited, Zerzura will be there, still to be discovered."

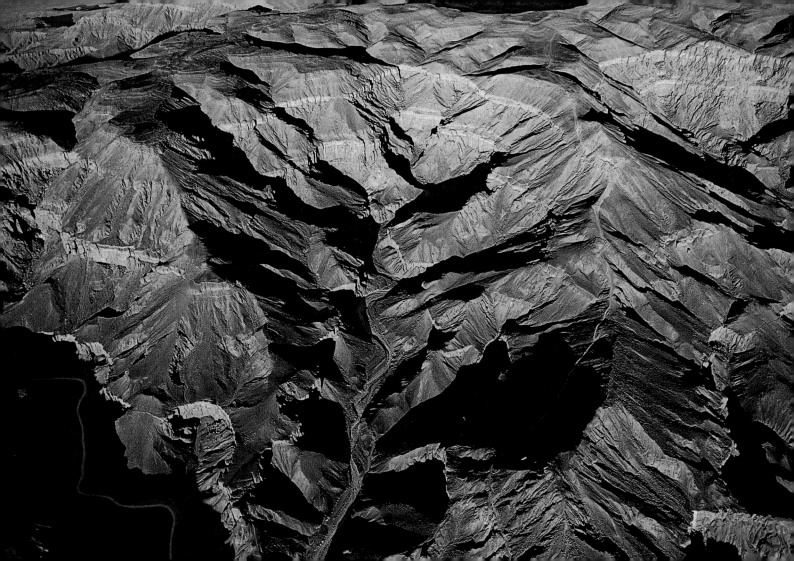

206 and 207
Rocky valleys and sand-filled depressions alternate in the desert east of the Valley of the Kings, on the west bank of the Nile near Luxor.

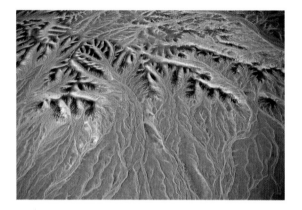

208 and 209
Near the Bahariya Oasis, rare but violent rains have etched the surface of the desert.

210-211
Near Bahariya, the great wadis, the desert valleys, are swept by the waters that collect in a network of hundreds of smaller channels.

212-213
The footprints of people and animals cross the sandy and rocky stretches of the White Desert near the Oasis of Farafra.

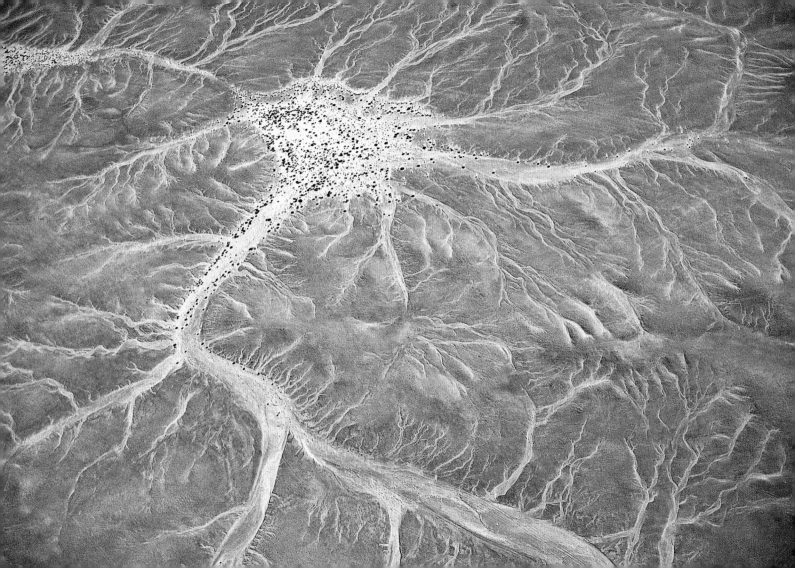

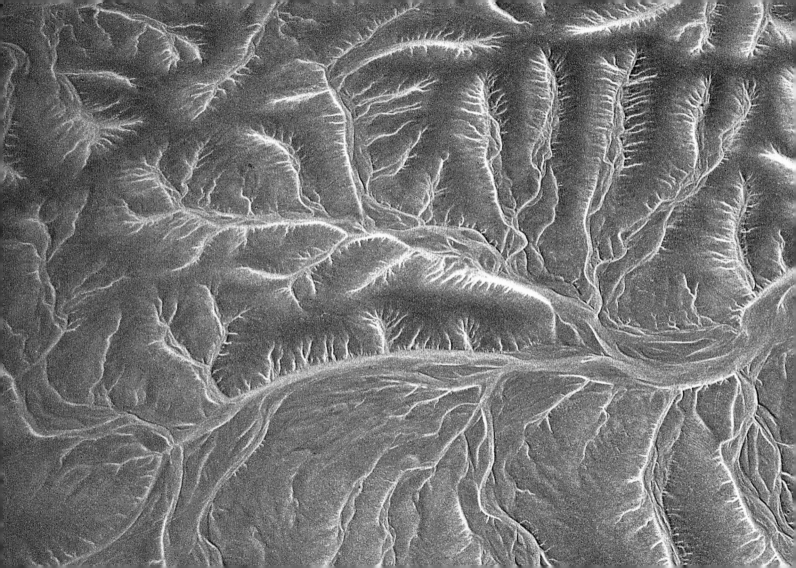

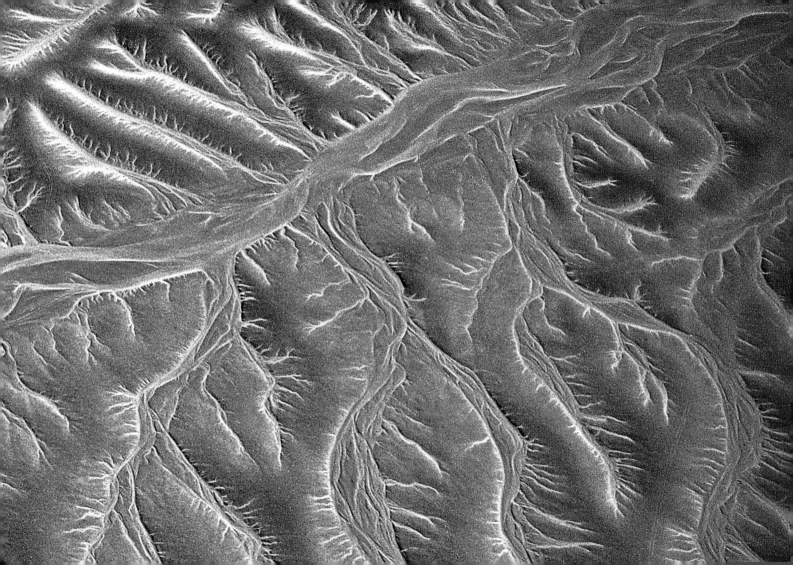

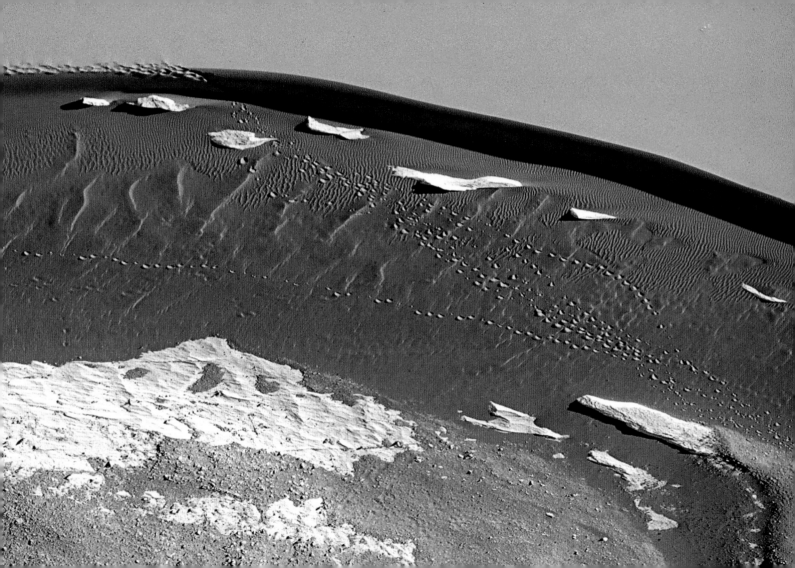

The deserts: the sands of Kemet

214 and 215
The White Desert of Farafra is named for the pale limestone formations that rise from the sand. The constant action of the wind has smoothed and rounded these stones.

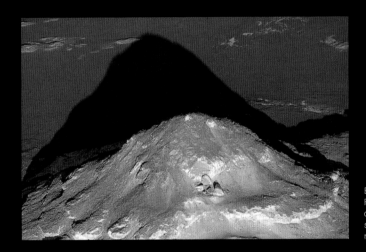

216 and 217
Every year, the White Desert of Farafra is visited by thousands of tourists, whose jeeps barely scratch the sandy surface surrounding the white rocks.

218 and 219

At dawn and sunset, the light makes the yellow sand stand out against
the brilliant white limestone composing the rocks of the White Desert.

220-221

Erratic apparitions in a bizarre desert, the rocks near Farafra create
bleak landscapes with an otherworldly aura.

222 and 223
The rocky floor of the White Desert emerges from the sand in the form of vast ridged surfaces or small outcrops.

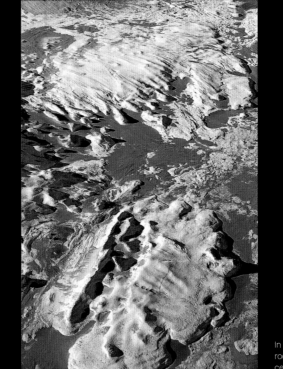

224 and 225
In the cold light of winter, the smooth rocks of the White Desert are reminiscent of a snow-covered countryside.

HIGH ABOVE EGYPT

227
Low, isolated hills shaped by the weather are all that remain
of the ancient surface of a stretch of desert near Farafra.

228-229
The Oasis of Fayum surrounds Lake Qarun, which was known as Lake Moeris in ancient times and was much larger than it is today.

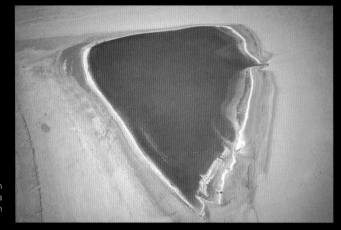

230, 231 and 232-233
Mineral deposits on the bottom of a small body of water create a splotch of color along the north shore of Lake Qarun.

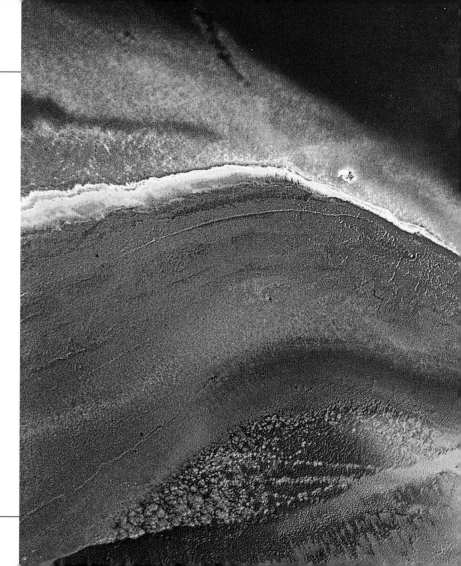

232-233
The lake once covered the desert along the shore of Birket Qarun, near Dimai, the location of this isolated body of water rich in mineral deposits.

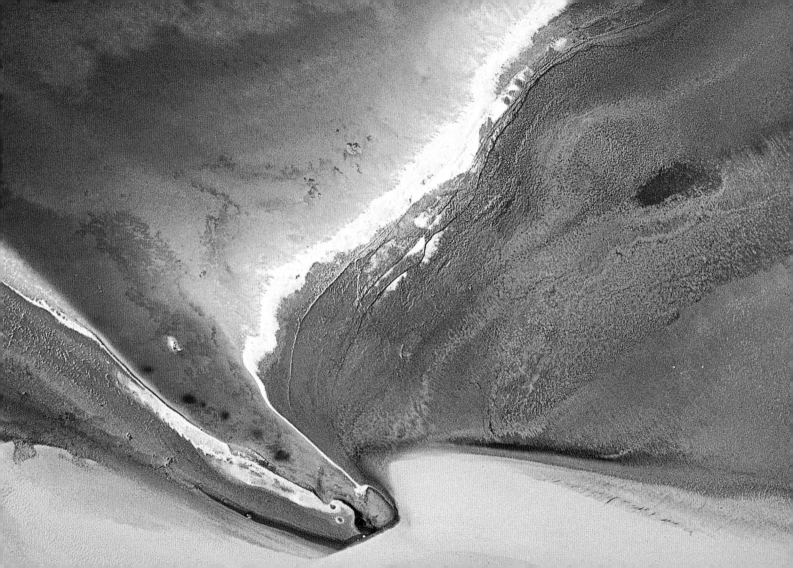

234 and 235
Lake Qarun must have had numerous crocodiles in the past, given the fact that the most important deity in this region under the ancient Egyptians was Sobek, the crocodile god.

236-237
A paved road snakes along the wadi that, farther up the valley, is the site of the large necropolis of the Valley of the Kings.

238-239
To the west, the panorama of the west bank of the Nile across from Luxor is closed off by a massive mountain chain.

240-241
The dazzling colors of a hot-air balloon stand out against the mountains west of Luxor.

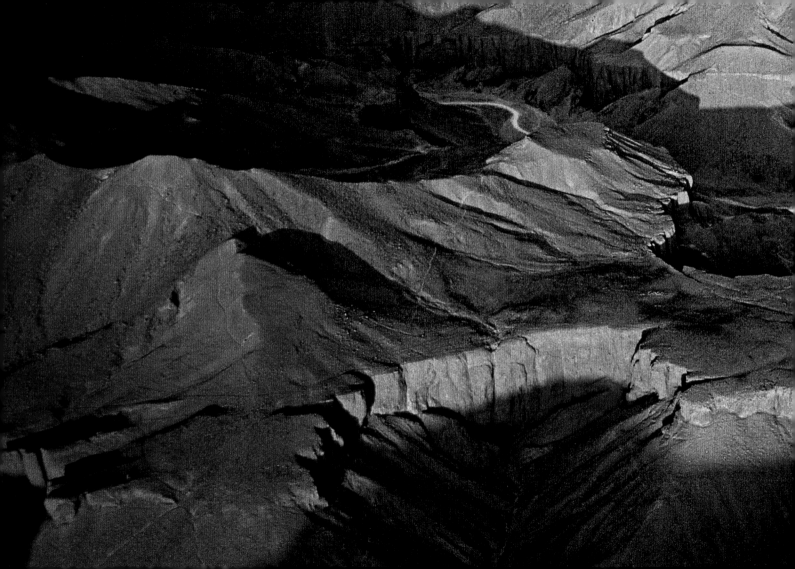

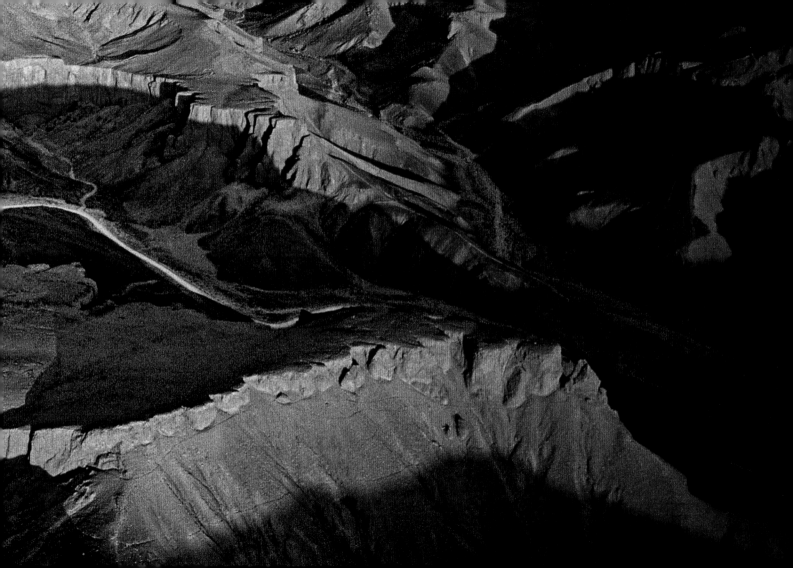

The deserts: the sands of Kemet

242 and 243
The mountains near Aswan are covered with a light layer of sand, which builds up in the surrounding valleys.

HIGH ABOVE EGYPT

245
Across from Aswan, the Monastery of St. Simeon rises in the desert, away from the lush, crowded banks of the Nile.

246-247
The Monastery of St. Simeon
near Aswan.

248 and 249
Sand and rock alternate along the shoreline of Lake Nasser, where a thin band of vegetation has appeared.

250
Long, slender strips of asphalt
cross the desert west of Lake
Nasser and lead to Abu Simbel.

251
New roads and the first signs of
irrigation meet along several
stretches of the desert shores of
Lake Nasser.

The
deserts:
the sands
of Kemet

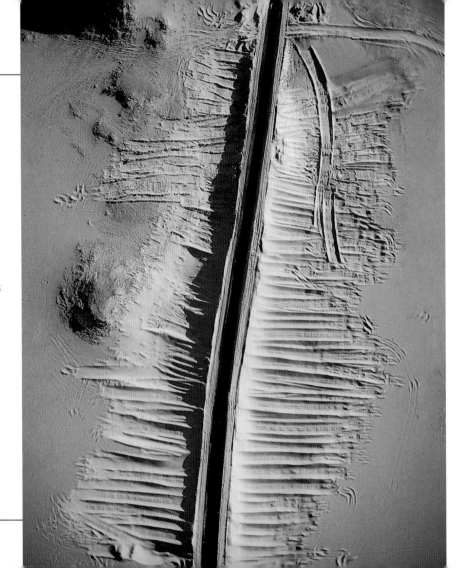

252
A paved road near Aswan still bears the scars of its construction.

253
Round dwellings with a central courtyard covered by a tent can be seen in the desert near Aswan.

254-255
Just a short distance from Lake Nasser, the presence of this large body of water is quickly forgotten as the desert stretches as far as the eye can see.

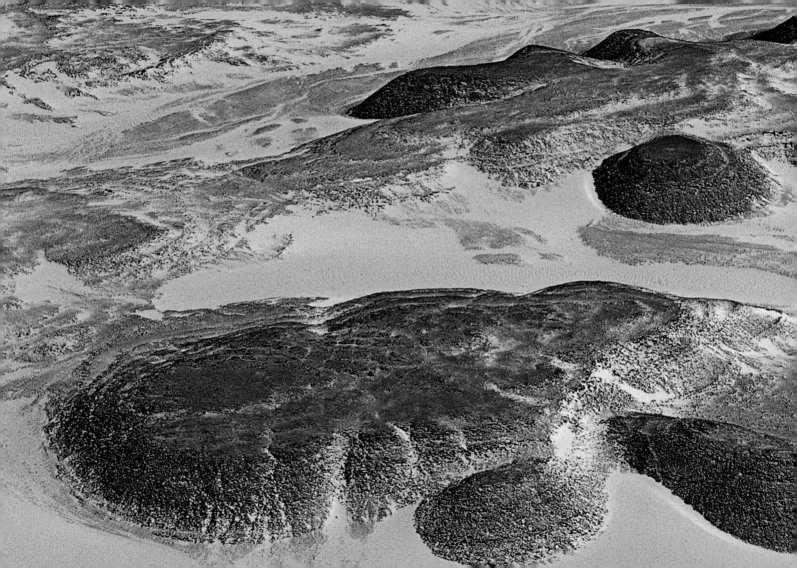

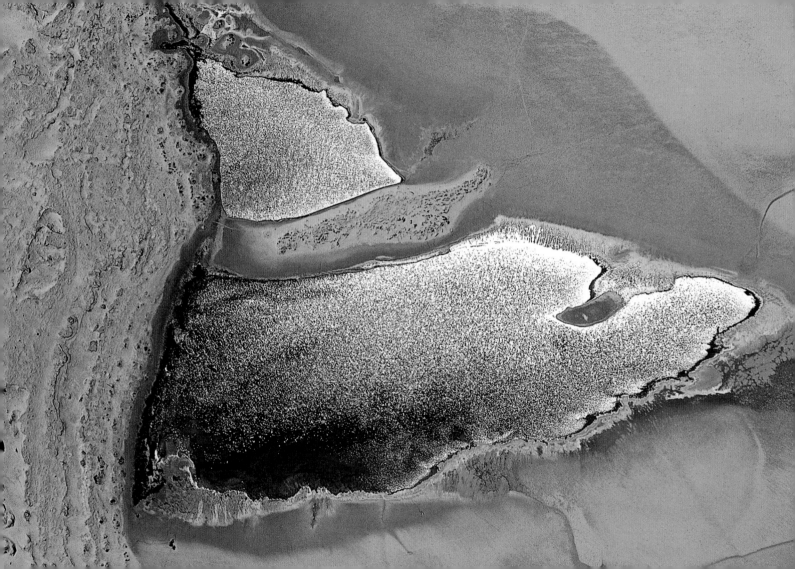

256 and 257
The depression of the Oasis of Siwa holds numerous bodies of water
in various shapes and sizes.

258 and 259
The interior of the Sinai Peninsula is occupied by mountain chains that rise to considerable heights, like the Gebel Serbal complex, crisscrossed by ancient watercourses that descend from the highest peaks to the lowest wadis around it.

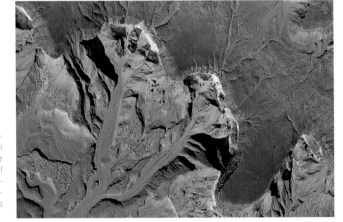

260 and 261
The wadis from the mountains behind Ras Gharib converge in a single broad plain that slopes gradually towards the Red Sea.

262-263
The Monastery of St. Catherine, built in a desert valley, is surrounded by scattered gardens of cypresses, olive trees and fruit trees.

264-265
The height of the mountains of the Sinai Peninsula varies from 2500 to 5000 feet, but there are several peaks that rise to over 6500 feet 800 to 1600 meters).

266 and 267 left
Views of the White Desert.

267 right
The waters of Lake Nasser bathe the Nubian Desert.

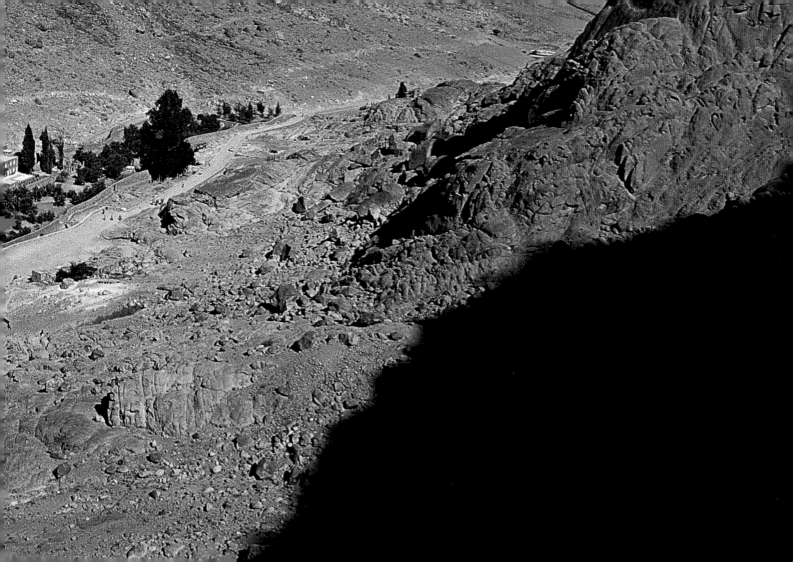

THE OASES
THE GIFT OF WATER

HIGH ABOVE EGYPT

269

The Monastery of St. Samuel (left) lies south of the sea of
vegetation of the Fayum Oasis (right).

As travelers leave the Nile Valley to head into the desert, they come across mountainous landscapes to the east and broad rippling expanses to the west, where rocks and sand reign supreme. Every so often, however, water reaches the surface to produce a number of oases, splashes of green—large and small—dotting the yellow desert. The lush vegetation of the largest oases covers dozens of square kilometers, while the smallest ones consist of a spring, a cluster of bushes, and a few palm trees.

Most of the oases have been inhabited—though not continuously—since ancient times. Explorations and recent studies have demonstrated that for several millennia, between 12,000 and 6,000 years ago, the climatic conditions were such that people were able to live in what is now an inhospitable desert. Dozens of archaeological sites dating to that period have been uncovered in Egypt and southern Libya, and every year new ones are discovered. When the climate became extremely arid again, prehistoric populations became concentrated around the oases and the Gilf Kebir. At a certain point, the Gilf was also abandoned and the large oases of the Western Desert remained the only "islands" inhabited by a stable population.

With the establishment of the powerful Egyptian state around 3000 B.C., the Nile Valley became the hub of the entire region. The oases thus became satellites of varying importance. The distribution of

270

Siwa is distinguished by a series of lakes whose
waters reflect the barren mountains around the oasis.

The oases: the gift of water

the population, concentrated around the few sources of water scattered across boundless desert areas, probably inspired Herodotus' epithet "Islands of the Blest" for the oases of the Western Desert. Four centuries later the geographer Strabo compared the region to a leopard skin, where the small inhabited areas were separated by sweeping arid and sandy expanses.

For the travelers of the past, human and animal alike, the oases were a respite after days of sun, wind, and sand, providing water, shade, and rest before they set out on the next leg of their journey. Several tiny oases, like Bir Dikka between Farafra and Dakhla, have never been more than a stopover. Some of the larger ones have had a checkered history. One example is Wadi Feiran in Sinai. A thriving settlement along the road to the Monastery of St. Catherine in the Byzantine period (third to seventh centuries A.D.), it was abandoned following the Arab conquest of 640–42 A.D. and was not reoccupied until the late nineteenth cen-

tury. Today, it houses a population of several hundred people and its lush palm grove is one of the area's most striking tourist attractions.

The history and development of the great oases of the Western Desert were profoundly influenced by their geographical position with respect to the Nile Valley. These are the Fayum, the closest one, which was virtually part of the great irrigation system of the region even in ancient times; Siwa, which is the farthest away and has maintained a different, independent character; little Bahariya, which received international attention following the recent discovery there of a Greco-Roman cemetery; rocky Farafra, surrounded by some of Egypt's most fascinating desert landscapes; and, lastly, Dakhla and Kharga, set against the backdrop of a spectacular escarpment. In ancient times, these two were considered a single, large oasis.

The Fayum differs from all the other oases as it is fed directly by the waters of the Nile coming from a canal that starts in the Asyut area. The pharaohs

The oases: the gift of water

of the Middle Kingdom became intensely interested in this area. As a result, they undertook major works to regulate the flow of water, draining marshes, moving the kingdom's capital city to the area, and building their pyramids in the desert between the oasis and the Nile Valley. The Fayoum also enjoyed a golden age under the Ptolemies (323–30 B.C.), thanks to its crops and the products from the lake, which was twice as large as it is today. The oasis became an important Christian center and by the thirteenth century, it had no less than thirty-five monasteries. After a long period of decline, the Fayoum flourished once again toward the mid-nineteenth century. Today, it is a highly populated region whose cultivated fields stretch as far as the eye can see.

Siwa, near the modern-day border with Libya, was not closely controlled by the Egyptian pharaohs until relatively late. In the sixth century B.C., the local temple dedicated to Ammon acquired great importance, and its oracle quickly became one of

the most important in the Mediterranean area. The attempt to subdue Siwa and destroy the oracle cost the Persian king Cambyses an entire army, defeated by the desert before it ever reached its destination. The fame of this sanctuary reached its zenith in 331 B.C. with the visit of Alexander the Great, who traveled to the oasis to consult the oracle. The oracle revealed that the young Macedonian leader, who had been crowned pharaoh of Egypt only a short time before, was descended from the gods, and it predicted the success of his military campaign in the east. Today, with its numerous lakes, famous palm trees laden with dates, and the impressive ruins of Aghurmi containing the remains of the Temple of Ammon, Siwa is one of the most fascinating oases in the area. And, of course, there is Shali, a millenary fortress built entirely of mud bricks and partly dissolved by the rains that battered the oasis in the 1920s. The outline and original appearance of this stronghold have been handed down to us through the draw-

275

The cultivated fields of the Fayum oasis extend as far as the
sands of the desert.

274

ings and descriptions of the travelers of the past. Bahariya, relatively close to the Nile Valley, prospered particularly during the Late Period and, above all, during the Greco-Roman era, as testified by the rich burials discovered only recently. The history of Farafra is far more obscure, and this oasis does not seem to have attracted much attention from either the pharaohs or the Romans. But it is surrounded by some of the most stunning desert scenery in Egypt. The White Desert, so called because of its landscape of pure white limestone with spectacular shapes rising from a carpet of ocher sand, is a natural wonder that attracts growing numbers of visitors every year. Equally dramatic is the passage to the west that leads to the little oasis of Ain Dalla, and to the Great Sand Sea beyond.

Farther south, the flat desert ends suddenly with a sheer cliff that surrounds two large oases, Dakhla and Kharga. Archaeological findings from the region show that Dakhla was an important settlement for the pharaohs as early as the Old King-

dom, and enormous resources were invested in the entire region during the late Roman era. At Kharga in particular, a chain of fortresses and fortified settlements was built to protect the crossroads of the important caravan routes passing through the area. The well-preserved remains of these impressive buildings mark one of the most spectacular local visitor attractions.

One of the most fascinating scenes in Dakhla is the Islamic settlement of al-Qasr, build entirely of mud bricks. Though no longer inhabited—the local population has moved to more modern dwellings in the area—al-Qasr has been restored in part and the town is virtually an outdoor museum. The maze of shady narrow streets twists amidst age-old buildings whose doors are decorated with antique architraves of carved wood. Here and there, stones with traces of Egyptian hieroglyphs can be glimpsed on a jamb or architrave, bearing witness to the long history of human settlement.

HIGH ABOVE EGYPT

276 and 277

In addition to the large lakes acting as a backdrop to villages and palm trees, the oasis of Siwa is also famous for its small springs, which rise from the depths of the soil and reach the surface in large pools rimmed by vegetation.

278-279

Modern towns and the ruins of ancient ones rise like islands from Siwa immense and luxuriant palm groves.

280

At Siwa, the violent rains of 1926 literally melted the mud-brick fortress of Shali.

281

Gebel al-Mawta, the Mountain of the Dead, is pitted with Siwa's ancient cemeteries.

282-283

The ancient buildings of Siwa, made of mud bricks and reinforced with palm trunks, were built on several levels. Today, they have been abandoned in favor of modern constructions.

284
Little remains of the temple devoted to Amun at Umm al-'Ibayda, which was part of the complex of the oracle temple at Siwa.

285
Dense palm groves surround the ruins of Aghurmi, which contain the remains of the oracle temple of Amun.

286 and 287
Siwa's lakes, which are quite salty, do not have any edible fish, and their waters permit the cultivation of only a limited number of products.

288 and 289
Patches of vegetation and cultivated plots have gradually taken over the land around the hills and waters of Siwa.

290 and 291
In Siwa, all that separates the desert from the lake waters is a slender strip of vegetation, with just a few bushes whose roots extend deep into the sand in search of water.

292-293
The dates produced by the immense palm groves of Siwa are considered among the best in North Africa and, together with olives, they represent the most important product of this oasis.

294 and 295
Encrustations of salt form in the lakes of Siwa, creating white webs that
stretch across the water.

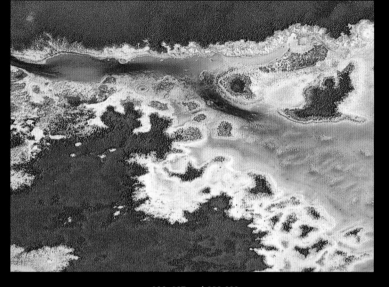

296, 297 and 298-299
For thousands of years, salt has accumulated in the depression of Siwa, forming white encrustations around its lakes.

300 and 301
A small Muslim cemetery covers a tiny patch of desert at the edge of the cultivated fields near Saqqara.

302

Cultivated fields now spread out beyond the original boundary of the valley and extend across the desert near Dahshur.

303

Modern irrigation has been tested in the plains of the desert of Helwan, south of Cairo, forming circular fields.

304-305

Near Saqqara, rows of white, pale blue, and sand-colored tombs begin under the shade of the palm trees at the edge of the fields and extend towards the desert.

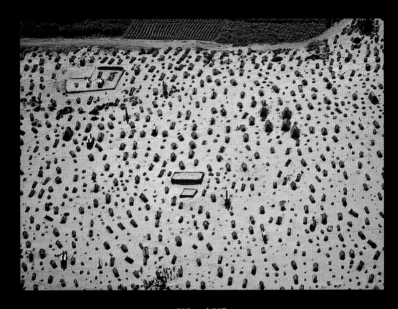

306 and 307
Large and small Muslims tombs dot a vast sandy area behind the
fields near Saqqara.

308 and 309

During the fourth century, the followers of one of the first and most influential hermits built the Monastery of St. Anthony in the hills of the Eastern Desert. Surrounded by tall walls, the monastery has its own spring and fields, making it virtually self-sufficient.

310 and 311
New roads and the outlines of fields to be cultivated are slowly covering the shores of Lake Qarun, in the Fayum oasis.

312-313
Fayum is now being expanded once again; in ancient times it was especially prosperous during the 12th Dynasty and the Greco-Roman Period, when cultivated fields covered a vast area.

The oases:
the gift
of water

314 and 315
The fields of Fayum and those of the Nile Valley are serviced by roads and canals, and they are dotted with towns and villages.

316 and 317
Although most crops come from relatively superficial cultivations, watermelons require parallel furrows that are over 6 feet (2 meters) deep. For years after the fields are abandoned, the furrows remain visible until sand gradually fills them completely.

318

The Monastery of St. Paul stands amidst the mountains of the Eastern Desert, just a few kilometers from the large Monastery of St. Anthony.

319

The Monastery of St. Samuel, in the southern part of Fayum, is served by two springs that make it possible to irrigate and cultivate a large area of land.

320 and 321
A modest lake brings life to the oasis of Bahariya and its main town Bawiti.

The oases:
the gift
of water

322 and 323
In the little oases of Bahariya, wind-borne sand overwhelms sponta-neous vegetation and cultivated fields alike.

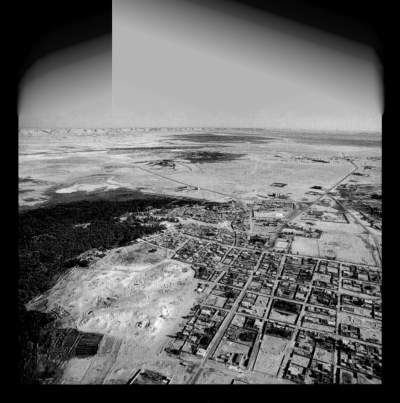

324 and 325
Even villages must defend themselves from the inexorable advance
of the desert sand, which covers and wipes out dwellings, fields, gar-

326-327
Qasr, the largest village in the oasis of Farafra, stands next to dense gardens irrigated by spring water.

328 and 329
The appearance of the oases of Fayum (shown in the two views on the left page) and Siwa (right) changes depending on the vantage point, light and time of day.

THE NILE
THE RIVER OF LIFE

HIGH ABOVE EGYPT

HIGH ABOVE EGYPT

Egypt and the Nile are indissolubly linked to each other, and it is impossible to discuss one without mentioning the other. Now, as in the past, this river is what distinguishes the narrow strip of highly fertile and habitable land from the vast deserts of sand and rock stretching as far as the eye can see along the sides of the valley.

The Nile we associate with the reign of the pharaohs corresponds to the northern portion of the world's longest river, formed farther south by three great tributaries, the White Nile, the Blue Nile, and the Atbara. The hydrographic basin of the Nile is immense, covering nearly three million square kilometers and reaching the great lakes of Central Africa.

The varied geographical and geological characteristics of the different areas that lie along the Nile have played a key role in the region's historical evolution. Virtually on a continuous basis, the ancient Egyptians controlled not only the valley between Aswan and Cairo, with its strips of fertile land varying in width, but also the Delta, whose arable land was double that of the Nile Valley. However, the most enterprising pharaohs always turned an expansionist eye toward the southern region of Nubia, poor in land but rich in gold and gemstones.

Thus, they conquered the area in several phases, particularly during the Middle Kingdom and the New Kingdom. Nevertheless, the Nile re-

The Nile: the river of life

mained the backbone of the Egyptian kingdom.

The river regulated and shaped the area, simply but powerfully. With its descent from south to north, the river gave the names of Upper and Lower Egypt to the lands it crossed, and it divided the landscape into two symmetrical halves: an east bank that looked toward the sunrise beyond a chain of mountain peaks, and a west bank where the sunset was symbolically evoked by the presence of the great royal necropolises.

The waters of the Nile not only irrigated the lands around it, they also formed the habitat of a wealth of spontaneous vegetation and a wide variety of animal species. The tombs of the New Kingdom in the area of ancient Thebes often have scenes portraying the family of the deceased enjoying a merry trip along the river, surrounded by butterflies and brightly colored birds soaring over thickets of papyruses and flowering plants, and fish in all shapes and sizes swimming just below the surface of the water. The men are portrayed as they fish or hunt, the women flaunt their finest attire and elaborate headdresses, and the children pick flowers or help their fathers hunt. In some cases, the group even includes the family cat, poised for a tidbit or busy frightening the nearby birds. However, not all the river's ancient denizens were peaceful: crocodiles and hippopotamuses, known for their ferociousness, were feared and respected. The former still thrive in Lake Nasser, behind the Aswan Dam, but the latter have completely disappeared from the region.

The wealth of Egypt, ancient and modern, has always been tied to the exploitation of its arable land, whose fertility depended largely on the reliable rhythm of the Nile. Until the construction of a series of dams, including the Aswan High Dam, the river regularly flooded the land along its banks from August through the end of September. After the waters receded, taking away harmful salts and leaving behind a layer of mud, the fields would be cultivated. Crops were harvested between Janu-

The Nile: the river of life

ary and April. The Nile would remain low until June, when the monsoon rains of Ethiopia and those of the Sudanese savannah would again swell its southern branches.

This cycle of regular flooding not only marked time with the annual rise and fall of the river, it also delimited space.

Herotodus noted that once the fields reemerged from the water, they had to be measured again to reestablish their borders. According to the Greek historian, this process of measuring the land gave rise to "geo-metry," in the oldest and most literal sense of the term. Invented on the banks of the Nile, this art eventually reached Greece, where it became the pride of generations of illustrious thinkers.

The Nile, tamed by dams and canals, now flows peacefully in its bed bordered by dense vegetation. Long the country's most important thoroughfare, the Nile is traveled by boats of all sizes. Bridges cross the river at only a few points, so ferries or sailboats are generally used to get from one side to the other. Traditional feluccas, boats with a triangular sail, dot the tourist areas in particular, where they are also used for short excursions along the river.

Starting in the mid-nineteenth century, tourists arriving in Egypt would board a sailing ship in Cairo and travel even as far as Wadi Halfa, in modern-day Sudan. Today, cruises along the Nile are still popular, but they take place on large motor vessels with several decks, which generally travel between Luxor and Aswan. The classic cruise stops at some of Egypt's most famous monuments, from the Temple of Karnak and the Valley of the Kings to the Ptolemaic temples of Edfu and Kom Ombo, going as far as the islands of Philae and Elephantine.

A smaller number of cruises is also organized above the High Dam on Lake Nasser, where a handful of boats glide over still waters to the Temple of Abu Simbel.

The Nile: the river of life

336-337
The city of Damietta is outlined along the horizon. After covering 4,145 miles (6,690 kilometers), the world's longest river flows into the Mediterranean.

338-339 and 340-341
Every piece of land around the Nile—here at Mit Abu Ghalib, in the Delta—is exploited for cultivation.

342
About 2500 years ago, Herodotus referred to the triangle of 8,500 square miles (20,000 square kilometers), around the mouths of the Nile as the "delta," because its shape resembled the Greek letter of that name.

343
The east branch of the Nile flows into the Mediterranean near the ancient city of Damietta, now a major port, located on Lake Manzala.

344-345
The modern expansion of Damietta occupies the west bank of the last segment of the river before it flows into the sea.

346, 347 and 348-349
In addition to the branches into which the Nile divides naturally, the Delta is also furrowed by numerous artificial canals that help channel water through cultivated fields.

The Nile: the river of life

350-351
The small settlements in the area of Shiribin in the Nile Delta lie along riverbanks and are surrounded by fields.

352-353
Near Damietta, in the eastern Delta, shellfish are farmed in large fenced pools.

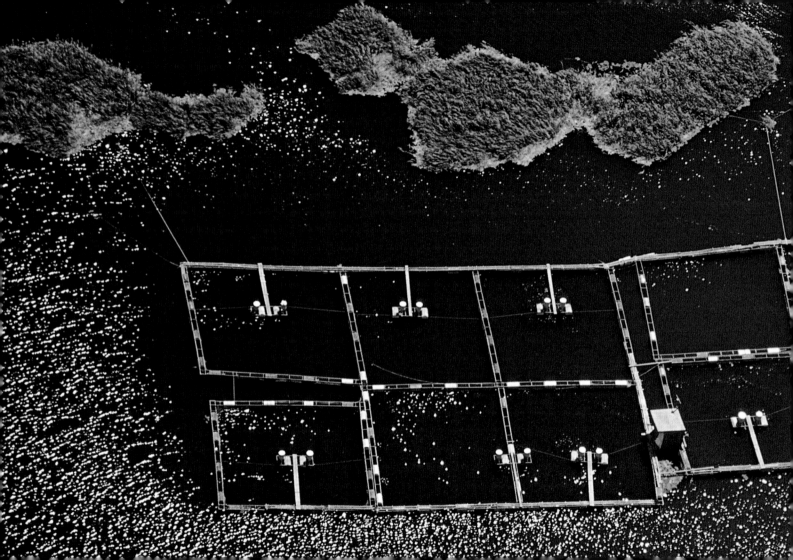

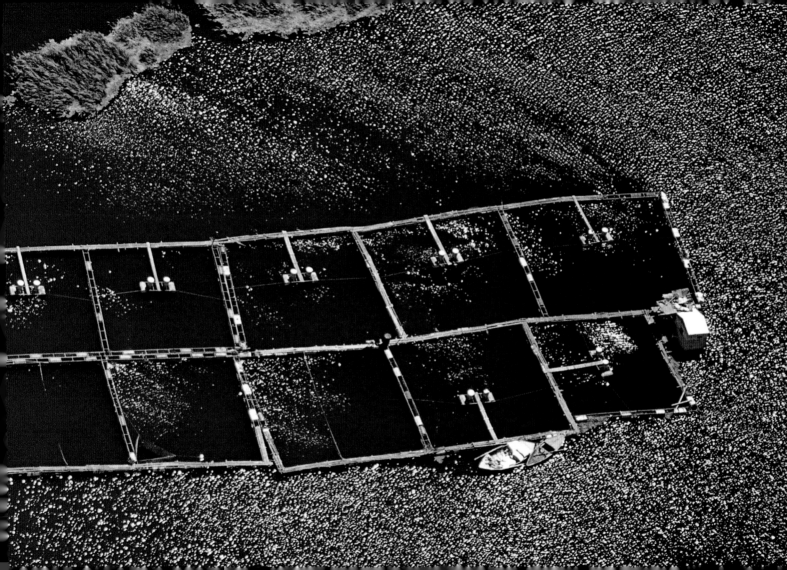

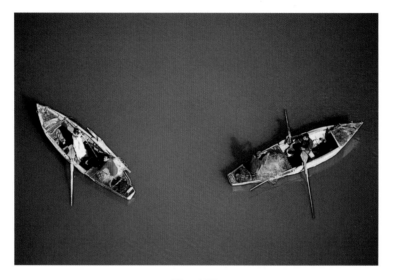

354 and 355
Every day, small and large rowboats and sailboats cross Lake Manzala
with groups of fishermen aboard.

The Nile: the river of life

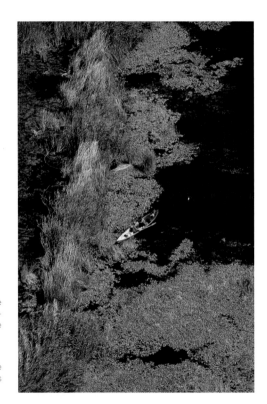

356 and 357
Fishermen push their boats into the marshes covered with dense vegetation around Lake Manzala, in the Nile Delta.

358-359
Vast "islands" of vegetation speckle the waters of Lake Manzala with countless shades of green.

360 and 361
The little port of al-Matariya (right) on Lake Manzala hosts dozens of small boats used regularly by the local fishermen (left).

362-363
Small clusters of fishing boats cross Lake Manzala in search of fish.

The Nile:
the river
of life

364 and 365
The most common boats on Lake Manzala have small triangular sails anchored
to a beam fastened to the mast.

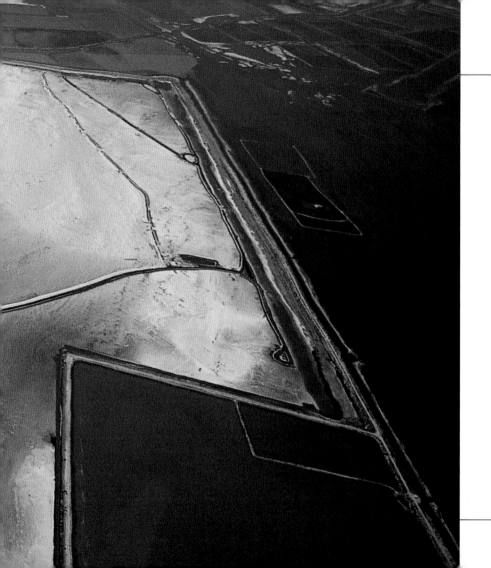

366-367
The area around Damietta is full of mineral deposits, and their bright colors stand out against the green background of the fields.

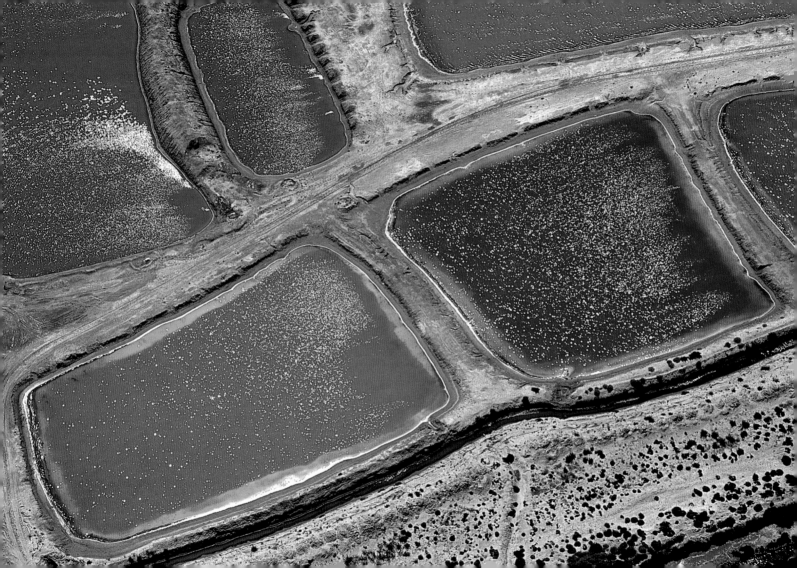

368, 369 and 370-371
Near Damietta, the dazzling colors of mineral extraction pools create
an enormous mosaic edged in white and set in the greenery of the
surrounding vegetation.

372 and 373
Luxurious homes gleam amidst the green palm trees and the cultivated rows near Cairo, close to the Nile. These residences were built
by well-to-do Egyptians, the modern "pharaohs" of a country that continues to develop.

The Nile: the river of life

374-375
The river flows peacefully south of Luxor, flanked by wide strips of cultivated fields.

376 and 377

Various crops are cultivated on plots of different shapes and sizes, creating mosaics of forms and colors like these near Luxor.

378-379

At Luxor, large tour ships dock in front of the temple, just a short distance from a group of large hotels and the market area.

380-381

The farmhouses in the Egyptian villages around Luxor are typically built with mud-brick walls and roofing made of wood and lightweight materials.

The Nile:
the river
of life

382-383
The donkey, alone or hitched to a cart, is the most common means of transportation used by Egyptian farmers to carry both people and goods.

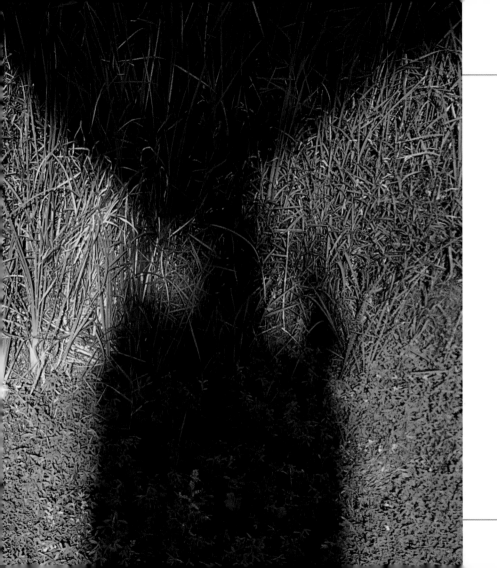

384-385
The shadow of the hot air balloon is outlined against the vegetation near the Nile, at Luxor, as a peaceful buffalo grazes obliviously.

 386

386 and 387
The camel and the donkey are sturdy animals. Nature has made them ideal as pack animals since the times of the ancient Egyptians, who also used them for the large caravans that crossed the desert.

388-389
From the silent vantage point of a hot air balloon, the sugarcane fields near Luxor create an evocative picture.

390-391
The glossy palm leaves and geo-metric shapes of the plots of land weave ornamental motifs across the fields.

392-393
Farmers, who have reached the fields with donkey-drawn carts, harvest their crops by hand near Luxor.

394 and 395
Farmers spend the entire day working in the fields with their donkeys.
Sometimes, men are accompanied by the entire family, which gathers
together at mealtimes.

396 and 397
Using a stick for leverage in the mud, a farmer in Luxor deftly maneuvers his boat through the low waters covered with vegetation.

The Nile:
the river
of life

398
In Egypt, no part of the palm tree goes to waste: dates are used as food, the leaves are used to weave mats and baskets, and the trunks are employed as building material.

399
Near Luxor, small villages expand towards the broad green stretch of crops, ending in an abrupt line – and only the desert lies beyond.

400
The sun rises east of Luxor. In the haze, the landscape towards the east is bare and flat as far as the eye can see, and
the Eastern Desert begins just beyond the river.

402-403
The early light of dawn is reflected in a double irrigation canal that brings water to the fields around Luxor.

The Nile:
the river
of life

Early in the morning, children go
to school along the paths that
wind their way through the fields
shaded by palm trees.

406 and 407
A dense sequence of fields extends along the west bank at Luxor, creating a contrast with the hot air balloon.

408
Just as the sun sets to the west behind the great mountain, the pharaohs ended their earthly journey in the tombs carved in the mountain on the west bank of Luxor.

409
The sun rises just behind Luxor during a thrilling hot air balloon flight.

410 and 411

Part of a small island near Luxor is occupied by a major hotel, where the various pavilions, swimming pools and tennis courts are set amidst trees, with the river and fields around them.

412-413

Groups of large tourist ships dock next to each other at the Luxor waterfront so travelers can visit the local monuments.

414 and 415
The banks of the Nile near Kom Ombo support dense palm groves, colorful plots of cultivated land, and densely populated towns that take on the color of the sand of the desert behind them.

416 and 417
The fertility of the soil along the Nile can clearly be seen in the wealth and variety of wild growth and crops covering the valley near Edfu.

418
A village near Esna has developed along the canal that brings water to meet the needs of its residents.

419
New canals and irrigation systems now make it possible to cultivate areas around Kom Ombo that were previously desert.

420-421
West of Kom Ombo, the cultivated strip narrows to a thin green band that follows the bank of the Nile.

422-423
Every day, large cruise ships sail along the Nile between Luxor and Aswan, passing in front of dozens of villages, towns, and pharaonic temples along the river.

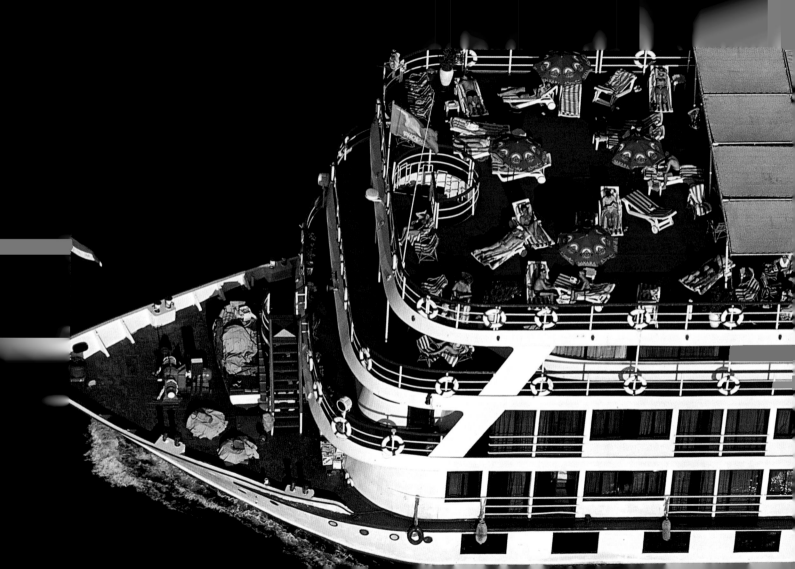

424-425
The cruise ships that take tourists along the river have restaurants, bars, swimming pools, and panoramic decks.

The Nile: the river of life

426-427
The outline of a village near Aswan seems to fade into the sands of the desert, which comes very close to the Nile at this point.

428-429
The Mausoleum of Agha Khan rises on the hill across from the island of Elephantine, behind which is the city of Aswan.

430 and 431
Feluccas with their distinctive triangular sails glide across the water between the banks of the Nile and the island of Elephantine, where archaeological remains from various eras are surrounded by dense, luxuriant vegetation.

The Nile: the river of life

432 and 433
The stretch of river across at Aswan is the perfect backdrop for short tours in traditional feluccas.

434-435

In the area around Aswan, the valley is narrower than it is in the northern part of the country, and the desert sands almost touch the river.

436-437
Near Aswan, tiny fields have been planted even in the very narrow green strip along the shore between the river and the sand.

HIGH ABOVE EGYPT

At the edge of Lake Nasser, desert and water meet—without
the interposition of the normal strip of vegetation.

440 and 441
Lake Nasser, which extends for over 310 miles (500 kilometers) into modern Sudan, was created by the construction of the High Dam, which rises to a height of about 330 feet (100 meters) and blocks the river about 12 miles (20 kilometers) south of Aswan.

The Nile: the river of life

442 and 443
The empty landscape surrounding Lake Nasser is slowly being transformed into a sweeping expanse of cultivated fields, thanks to new widespread irrigation systems.

444-445
The tops of ancient plateaus emerge from the silt-rich waters of Lake Nasser.

446-447
Hot-air balloon journey near Luxor.

THE CITIES
THE HUMAN LEGACY

HIGH ABOVE EGYPT

HIGH ABOVE EGYPT

449
The round towers of the Citadel of Cairo (left).
View of Alexandria (right).

Cairo, the capital of Egypt, is the country's largest and most important city, and one of the most densely populated cities in the world. The area now covered by the megalopolis has been populated since prehistoric times. Under the pharaohs, the town of On (in what is now the north-east of Cairo) was an important religious center later referred to by the Greeks as Heliopolis, but the city's true historical beginnings lie with the Roman fort of Babylon, part of whose towers and outside walls can still be seen today in Old Cairo. The city expanded as successive rulers built the mosques, tombs, and palaces that form part of the great city we see today. The mosques of Ibn Tulun and al-Azhar bear witness to the grandeur of the settlements built by the various dynastic rulers between the eighth and the thirteenth centuries. The Fatimids (969–1171 A.D.) completed great fortification works, the most evident traces of which are the monumental gates of Bab al-Futuh, Bab al-Nasr, and Bab Zuwayla, while the Citadel crowning the plain was the work of the military leader Salah al-Din al-Ayyubi (Saladin), who took command of Cairo after the Fatimid leadership went into decline. In the fourteenth century the market district of Khan al-Khalili, bounded on the east by the al-Husayn mosque, was built, and to this day, hundreds of little stores and shops selling jewelry, spices, glass, cotton, and handicrafts line the crowded streets, making up one of the city's favorite attractions.

Cairo's explosive development began in the late 1950s, with exponential population growth—in the or-

450
The monumental mosque of Mohammed Ali was built in
the fortified southern circle of the Cairo Citadel between
1830 and 1848.

The cities: the human legacy

der of millions of people—and urban expansion. Today, the skyline is dominated by dizzying skyscrapers, and the city also boasts a subway system. Cairo is surrounded by modern satellite cities, important industries, and suburban areas whose expansion seems boundless, but the heart of the metropolis is Tahrir Square, where the Egyptian Museum, the Arab League, several large hotels, and a number of important government buildings are located. The museum, which houses the largest and most important collection of artifacts from ancient Egypt, including the famous treasure from Tutankhamun's tomb, receives thousands of visitors every day. In the Nile is the island of Gezira, with its residential district of Zamalek, where many lovely villas of the last century have now been turned into foreign embassies. Skyscrapers and modern buildings line the riverbanks, where rows of houseboats and floating bars and restaurants are docked. From here, Cairo stretches infinitely toward both the east, where the airport is located, and the

west, where the metropolitan area has expanded as far as the pyramids of Giza.

Egypt's second largest city is Alexandria, which also boasts a glorious history. Founded by Alexander the Great in 331 B.C., it was the seat of the Ptolemaic dynasty (323–30 B.C.) until the last queen, Cleopatra, and her ally Mark Antony were defeated by Octavian. The fame of its celebrated library is rivaled only by that of the lighthouse that once stood at the entrance to the port. More than one hundred meters high and crowned by a statue of the sea god Poseidon, it was destroyed by an earthquake and its ruins were abandoned until the end of the fifteenth century, when the stones were reused to build a fortress that, even today, dominates the city shoreline.

Today, Alexandria is one of the chief ports of the Mediterranean. The importance of the fishing industry to the local economy is demonstrated by the enormous fish market located on the peninsula between the two bays. Although the city is home to many Islam-

The cities: the human legacy

ic monuments, it also has a European feel due to the villas and buildings constructed in the nineteenth century by the large foreign population that moved there. The new library—the Bibliotheca Alexandrina—is the city's most important modern building. This unusual round construction has a roof composed of a series of skylights tilted toward the sea.

The opening of the Suez Canal in 1869 influenced the development of the cities of the Nile Delta. Suez, first an ancient Ptolemaic and then a Roman city, is now a major industrial center. Port Said and Ismailiya are "daughters" of the canal; the former was established when work began on the canal, while the latter was founded as a depot for the builders of the canal. Dumyat, or Damietta, has lovely buildings from the Ottoman period. Located on the banks of Lake Manzala, it too has benefited from the proximity of the canal, and has now become a large industrial port.

In recent years, the Red Sea coast has come to be associated almost wholly with the tourist trade, and the development of many towns there is due entirely to the growing presence of Egyptian and foreign visitors. Enormous investments have transformed small villages into crowded resorts, likewise creating vast hotel complexes where virtually nothing had stood before. On the Sinai Peninsula, Sharm al-Sheikh has developed from a village to an important city in just a few years, with the addition of various residential districts and countless hotels. The area of Na'ama Bay in particular—a complex of hotels, shopping centers, and services—has now become nothing short of a fashionable little city in its own right. Similarly, new major hotels and residences in El Gouna have greatly increased the number of tourist accommodations in the area around Hurghada. The popularity of the city of Marsa Matruh is also growing. Located on the Mediterranean coast west of Alexandria, the city is surrounded by long, unspoiled beaches.

Returning to the valley, cities and villages along the Nile alternate with cultivated fields against the

455
The early light of dawn illuminates the tallest buildings of Luxor and reaches the great mountain that rises on the west bank. Hidden behind the mountain is the Valley of the Kings.

backdrop of the desert beyond. The main cities are Minya, which is home to a large Coptic community, and Asyut, which boasts the remains of several buildings from the Mamluk period. Upstream, the course of the river curves broadly to the east, thus drawing closer to the Red Sea. The most important cities in this area are located at the start of ancient caravan routes, which have now been converted into paved roads that cross the Eastern Desert. One example is Qena, at the start of the road that leads to the coast at Safaga; another is Qift, the ancient city of Coptos, the starting point for the road that crosses Wadi Hammamat. Travelers of all eras have left graffiti and inscriptions on the rocks along the sides of this narrow passage through the mountains.

Luxor and Aswan are the two most important cities of Upper Egypt. The development of Luxor as a city is due largely to its proximity to the ruins left behind by the pharaohs, which attract visitors from every corner of the world. Until the early nineteenth century, when the historic and archaeological impor-

tance of this area became known, Luxor was just one of many villages along the Nile. Today, after two centuries of archaeological excavation and millions of visitors, it has become a densely populated city with an airport, railroad, major hotels, and wharves for docking cruise ships.

The very ancient origins of Aswan and its importance in the various historical periods are due to its strategic position downstream from the first cataract, a natural barrier that marked the southern boundary of ancient Egypt for years. The archaeological sites that have been discovered in the area are one of Aswan's leading attractions, though the spectacular landscape around it also adds to its charm. The river here is dotted with a myriad of islands of all sizes, edged in massive granite boulders and covered with rich vegetation, and feluccas and small ferries glide slowly between them. Beyond the bend in the river is the immense High Dam that has harnessed the waters of the Nile since 1970, creating a vast body of water—Lake Nasser—behind it.

Cairo

458
The American University in Cairo occupies a large complex of buildings at the corner of Tahrir Square, in the heart of the city.

459
Tahrir Square, where the Egyptian Museum is located, is lined with a number of important hotels.

460 and 461
The Cairo Museum, built in the early twentieth century, currently houses artifacts from the Predynastic Period up to the Greco-Roman period, including the treasure of Tutankhamun.

462
The minaret of Masgid al-Fath, the tallest in the world, stands out against the background of Ramses Square.

463
Until the 1950s, the island of al-Roda was essentially a rural area, but today it has become a crowded central district of Cairo.

HIGH ABOVE EGYPT

465
The little palace of Munastirli, which covers the southern tip of the island of al-Roda, was built in the mid-nineteenth century on the site of an ancient mosque dating back to the eleventh century.

466
The area once occupied by the Roman fort of Babylon, where the Copts built a number of churches and monasteries, is now virtually an extensive outdoor museum.

467
A modern Coptic church in a residential district of Cairo.

468 and 469

The outline of the Citadel is dominated by the Mosque of Mohammed Ali, known also as the Alabaster Mosque due to the fact that its interior is finished with this stone.

Cairo

470

Two colossal mosques rise at the feet of the Citadel, the Mosque of Sultan Hasan, with its central courtyard and the enormous dome at the back, and the Mosque of al-Rifa'i.

471

The Fatimids built the Mosque of al-Azhar at the end of the tenth century, but the enormous complex has been modified and expanded continuously over the centuries.

472
The Mosque of Sayyidna el-Husayn is one of the most important in Cairo. It was built during the nineteenth century over the place where al-Husayn, one of Mohammed's grandchildren, is buried.

473
The dense urban fabric of old Cairo is broken up by the great Mosque of al-Hakim, built by the Fatimids at the beginning of the eleventh century.

474-475
The great Eastern Cemetery has been used since the fifteenth century. It is also referred to as the "City of the Dead" because many tombs are used as dwellings by families who have nowhere else to go.

476 and 477
The Western Cemetery is older than the Eastern one. Because of its historic importance, it was chosen as the burial place for many important figures from the Ottoman period.

478-479
Views of Cairo.

481
The Mosques of Abu al-Abbas al-Mursi and Sidi Busiri are just a short distance from the beachfront of Alexandria, which extends seaward along a narrow peninsula.

Alexandria

482 and 483
The squared lines of the buildings along the Alexandria beachfront contrast with the curved domes of the Mosques of Sidi Busiri and Abu al-Abbas al-Mursi.

484-485

A narrow strip of land and a mole protect the northern portion of Alexandria's East Port, once dominated by the famous lighthouse.

486

Built by Sultan Qaytbay in the fifteenth century, one of the two fortresses defending the East Port rose over the ruins of the lighthouse, which collapsed in 1307 due to an earthquake.

488
Most of the Greco-Roman city of Alexandria where Cleopatra lived has been submerged by the sea. It lies underwater offshore from the modern city.

489
The roofing of the circular building housing the modern library of Alexandria is composed of a series of skylights and is tilted towards the sea.

490-491
A natural barrier creates a series of lagoons between the city of Marsa Matruh and the Mediterranean Sea.

Damietta

492-493
Damietta owes its historical importance to its strategic position near the mouth of the eastern branch of the Nile.

Rosetta

494-495
Rosetta, set at the mouth of the
western branch of the Nile, was
the symmetrical counterpart of
Damietta, but it was later over
shadowed by the importance of
Alexandria.

Suez

496-497
Impressive excavation work and channeling has shaped the coastline near Suez into a geometric passageway to service canal operations.

498 and 499
The southern end of the Suez Canal flows into the Gulf of Suez, past
the modern city of Suez. Farther north, it is flanked by a snaking canal.

500 and 501
Large cruise ships spend a few days lined up in orderly rows along
the east bank of Luxor as travelers visit the numerous archaeological
sites that have made this location one of Egypt's most important
tourist destinations.

502 and 503
The modern city, edged by a tree-lined avenue along the river, surrounds the temple of Luxor and stretches north towards the complex of Karnak.

Luxor

504 and 505
Across from Luxor, the west bank of the Nile is dotted with little villages, while isolated farmhouses can be seen between the fields.

HIGH ABOVE EGYPT

507
Dawn over a farm village on the west bank of the Nile near Luxor.

508
During a funeral, women dressed in black gather before a farmhouse in the village of al-Qurna, on the west bank across from Luxor.

510 and 511
The Coptic community that lives on the west bank of Luxor has a number of centers, including the Monastery of St. Theodore, whose entrance is indicated in Arabic, English, and Coptic.

512 and 513
Around Luxor, there are buildings constructed according to tradition, with nearly every room covered by a small dome, while modern buildings in reinforced concrete and bricks are generally flat-roofed.

Aswan

514 and 515
A village near Aswan has an array of mud-brick houses covered with vaults and domes, and arranged around inner courtyards.

516 and 517
The city of Aswan and the Mausoleum of the Agha Khan face each other across the Nile, which flows here amidst a multitude of rocky islands covered with vegetation.

518
Some of the small islands at Aswan have been colonized by large hotel complexes complete with swimming pools. The hotels use private ferries to connect them to the city.

519
The Old Cataract is one of Aswan's most famous hotels. It was the setting for Agatha Christie's book *Death on the Nile*, as well as the movie based on the book.

520

The garden and swimming pool of the Old Cataract directly overlook the Nile, over a row of little embarcaderos for feluccas and motorboats.

521

A small hotel with a swimming pool and garden lined with palm trees rises on the rocky spur of an island south of Elephantine, across from Aswan.

522-523

Around the millenary archaeological remains found on the island of Elephantine, the river, islands, vegetation, feluccas, and modern towns create a fascinating landscape of rare beauty.

524 and 525
Large tourist complexes are being built around Hurghada, transforming what was once a desert area into a densely populated zone with parks, swimming pools, and playing fields.

Hurghada

526 and 527
Large tourist resorts have colonized the shores of Hurghada, redesigning the coastline by building small towns or creating beaches and interior lagoons.

528 and 529
Hurghada continues to expand rapidly to accommodate tourism, thanks also to its virtually inexhaustible stretches of panoramic coastlines.

530 and 531
The landscape of El Gouna, near Hurghada, is dotted with lagoons, and it has proven to be ideal for building tourist resorts separated from each other by canals and bodies of water.

532 and 533
El Gouna, a tourist complex established just a few miles north of Hurghada, is composed of numerous hotels that have been designed to make the most of the layout of the coastline and the area's breathtaking landscape.

Sharm al-Sheikh

534

The town of Sharm al-Sheikh is located just a few miles south of Na'ama Bay, near a pair of bays, one of which has a popular small harbor.

535

Strict apportionment of the valuable territory of Na'ama Bay has been combined with architectural solutions that follow the natural layout of the coast and make the most of its surface area.

Sharm al-Sheikh

536-537
The large hotels rising along the beachfront of Na'ama Bay in Sinai vie with each other to display the complex geometries of their buildings and gardens.

538
Several hotels at Sharm al-Sheikh opt for pools with geometric shapes, while others attempt to recreate the effect of a natural lagoon by creating pools with undulating, uneven shapes.

539
The hotel complexes of Sharm al-Sheikh and Na'ama Bay can accommodate enormous numbers of tourists.

Dahab

540 and 541
Dahab has maintained its un-spoiled beauty, attracting tourists and travelers who want a natural setting.

542-543
Dahab, a charming town over-looking the Gulf of Aqaba, at-tracts numerous divers, who ap-preciate the rich marine environ-ment.

THE RED SEA AND THE MEDITERRANEAN SEA

HIGH ABOVE EGYPT

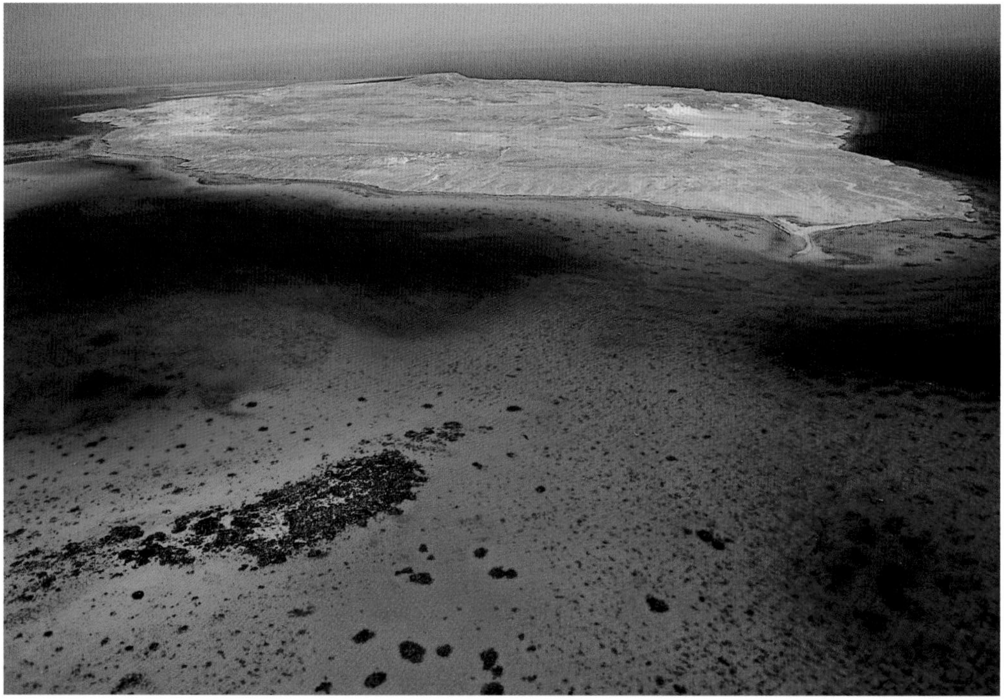

545

A shipwreck on the Mediterranean coast near Idku, between
Rosetta and Damietta (left). The coral reef across from
Hurghada (right).

Egypt is bathed by two seas. To the north is the Mediterranean, into which the Nile and its great Delta flow, and to the east is the Red Sea, located between Egypt and Saudi Arabia, and closed off by the Sinai Peninsula to the north.

Low and sandy, the northern coast of Egypt toward Libya is bounded by the pale yellow desert and the turquoise sea. In 1942, this peaceful landscape was the scene of one of the fiercest battles of the Second World War. The final battle for control of the African coast was waged at el-Alamein, one hundred kilometers west of Alexandria, pitting the Allies against Italian and German troops. Today, a cemetery and several memorials commemorate the tens of thousands of soldiers killed or missing in action.

The landscape is transformed into a dazzling lagoon on the coastline of the Nile Delta, crowned by a sequence of enormous salt lakes where the waters of the Nile meet the sea. The largest of these, Lake Manzala, is an enormous mosaic of vegetation in every shade of green, gleaming against the blue sea.

Near this lake, the Suez Canal joins the Mediterranean. The northern mouth of this important maritime corridor, which partially exploits a series of natural lakes, is marked by the city of Port Said, while the city of Suez is situated at its southern outlet. The pride of modern Egypt, the canal actually has a long history. In the sixth century B.C., during the period of the Twenty-sixth Dynasty of the pharaohs, an

546

A small desert isle lies in the Red Sea near the
island of Tiran.

The Red Sea and the Mediterranean Sea

attempt was made to link the Mediterranean and the Red Sea for military and trade purposes; 2,400 years later, the very same reasons inspired the Egyptians and the French to tackle the colossal undertaking, which was completed in 1869. Great Britain also benefited from the canal, as it provided a vital shortcut for the country's trade with India.

The Red Sea has been used since the days of the pharaohs as a trade corridor. As early as the Old Kingdom in the third millennium B.C., the Egyptians imported gold, ebony, ivory, and exotic plants and animals from a land they called Punt, which was probably in the area corresponding to modern-day Sudan and Eritrea. Portrayals of these shipments discovered in the tombs and temples of the New Kingdom demonstrate that much trade was handled using large ships that, laden with valuables, followed the coastline of the Red Sea. The Romans also exploited the Red Sea for trade purposes, utilizing a series of ports initially established during the Ptolemaic period. The most important was Berenike, which was connected to the Nile Valley by a caravan route with military surveillance and wells along the way. Laden with olive oil, wine, metal, and coral, the Roman ships set sail from Berenike for Ethiopia, Somalia, and India, returning with ivory, myrrh, aromatic plants, gemstones, pearls, and ultrafine cotton.

Because of its pale sand, turquoise waters, and spectacular coral reefs, the Red Sea coast has now become one of the country's chief tourist attractions. Enormous investments have transformed what were small villages only a few years ago into large towns devoted entirely to tourism. For years, spots like Sharm al-Sheikh on the Sinai Peninsula and Hurghada have been traditional destinations for enormous numbers of visitors, Egyptian and foreign alike. In the wake of the success enjoyed by the Sinai Peninsula and the northern coast, urbanization to cater to tourists has proceeded inex-

The Red Sea and the Mediterranean Sea

orably southward. It has now reached Marsa Alam, which until recently was just a small village that marked the coastal endpoint of a long road starting in the valley and crossing the Western Desert.

The underwater landscape of the Red Sea is undoubtedly one of the most beautiful in the world. Corals of every shape and color stand out clearly in the azure water, providing a backdrop to the movement of enormous schools of colorful fish. This extraordinary display attracts thousands of divers every year. The intensive exploitation of the Sinai area for tourism prompted the establishment of several protected areas, where land and marine flora and fauna can thrive undisturbed. Extending west of Sharm al-Sheikh is the natural reserve of Ras Mohammed, the southernmost tip of the Sinai Peninsula. It includes a rocky headland and the portion of the coral reef that extends from here into the sea depths. Another protected area has been established at Nabq, northeast of Sharm al-Sheikh, around a lagoon covered by a forest of mangroves, an aquatic plant whose leaves expel salt absorbed from seawater. At the Nabq lagoon, a veil of water—through which the light sand of the desert is visible—surrounds low islets covered with vegetation. These small islands are the habitat of numerous animal species, including various migratory birds. Because of the currents and the coral reef, the waters of the Red Sea can be difficult to navigate. The coastline is dotted with wrecks, some quite large, testifying to the tragic shipping accidents that, in some cases, cost many lives. Some of the wrecks are grounded on the shallow floors of the reef, battered by the wind and waves, while others rest at the bottom of the sea. There are also the remains of many ships that sank during the Second World War. The most famous, the Thistlegorm, still holds its cargo of motorcycles, cars, and trucks. Shoals of fish now dart amidst these coral-encrusted vehicles in the silent blue depths of the sea.

Mediterranean Sea

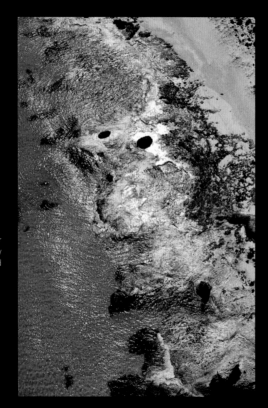

550 and 551
The pristine Mediterranean coast near the city of Marsa Matruh winds its way through pale sand, dark boulders and the sapphire sea.

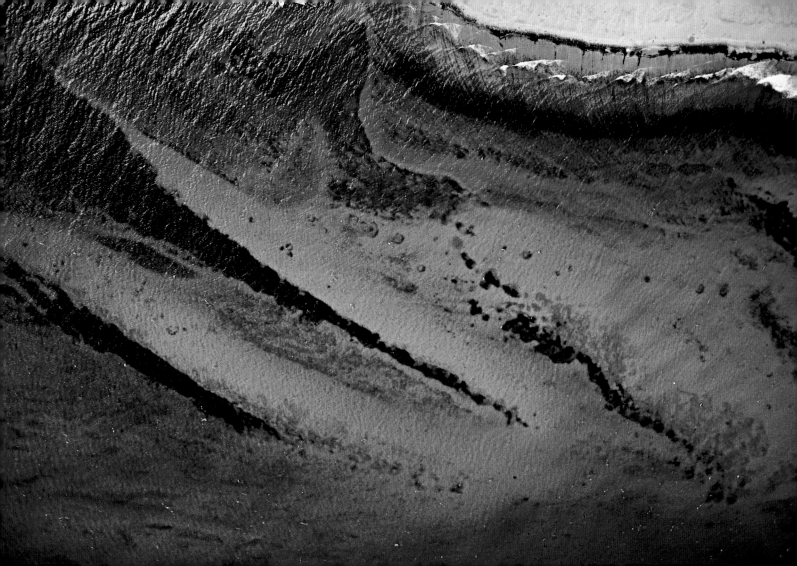

552
Starkly outlined rocks rise from the clear waters of the Mediterranean Sea along the coast west of Alexandria.

554 and 555

The coast between Alexandria and Marsa Ma-truh hosts a series of tourist resorts that take advantage of the sinuous line of the sandy peninsulas that stretch into the sea, creating pools and lagoons.

556-557

Natural barriers create shallow bodies of water in front of Marsa Matruh, set on the Mediterranean coastline.

558 and 559
Near Marsa Matruh, the German War Memorial (left) and the Italian one (right) honor the thousands of soldiers who lost their lives between September 1940 and March 1943.

560 and 561
Like the coast of the Red Sea, the Mediterranean shoreline has been fatal for passing ships, as demonstrated by the partially submerged shipwrecks near both Alexandria and Idku.

562-563
Currents and the shallow sea floor evidently betrayed the ship that ran aground near Idku. Its remains lie abandoned, battered by the wind and waves.

564-565
Rolling waves break on the sandy Mediterranean shores of Egypt.

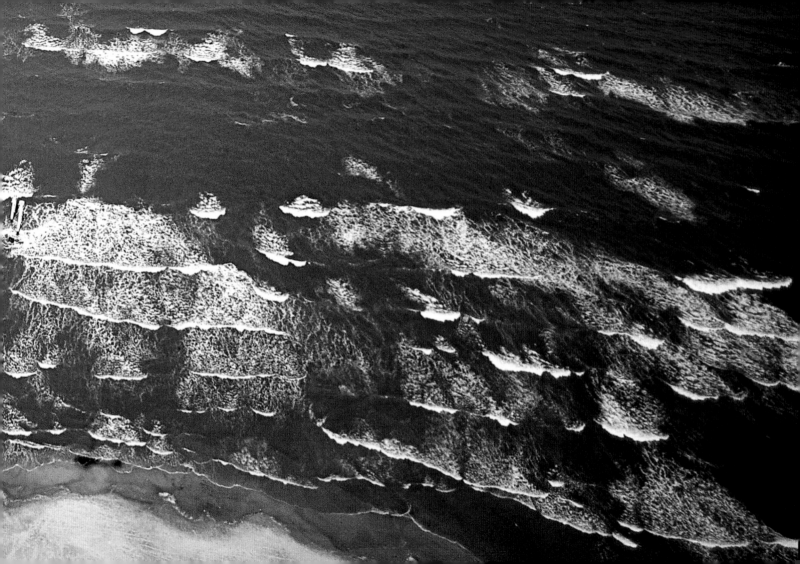

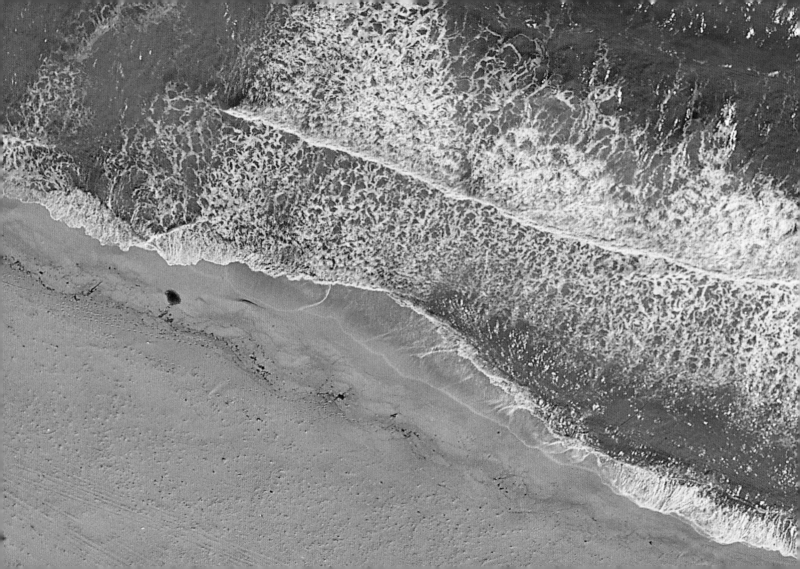

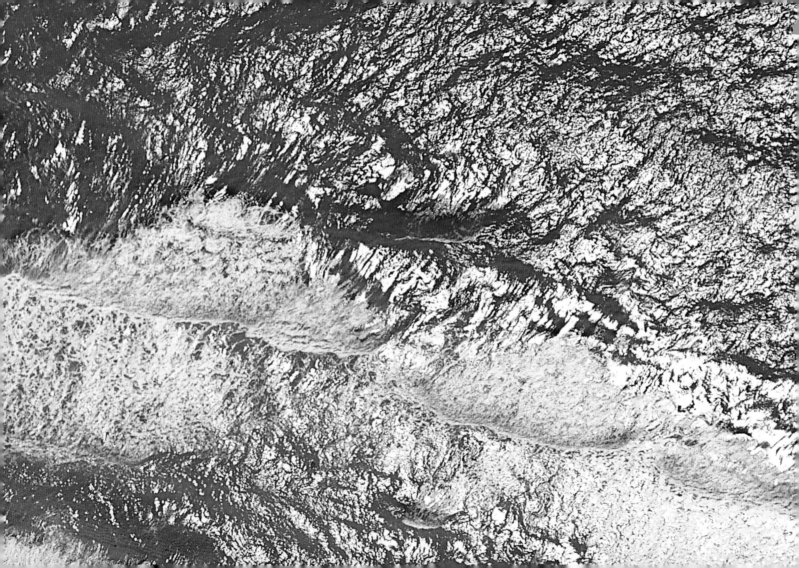

Red Sea

566 and 567
Broad coral reefs fan out just below the surface of the water near the Strait of Tiran, in the southern Sinai Peninsula, and along the Strait of Gubal.

568
The Strait of Gubal marks the southern entrance to the arm of the sea known as the Gulf of Suez, which then leads to the Suez Canal.

570-571
A solitary boat—tiny on the glistening sea—sails near Hurghada. The photograph offers an idea of the sheer vastness of these places, which attract thousands of visitors every year.

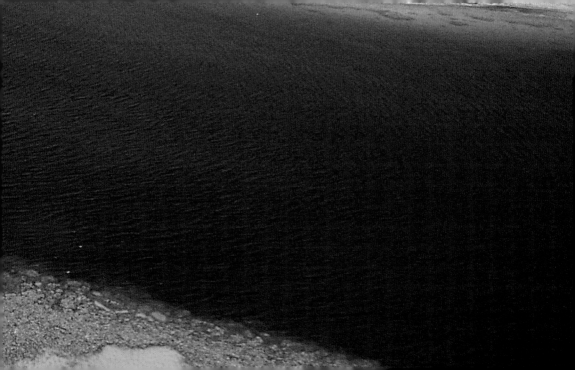

Red
Sea

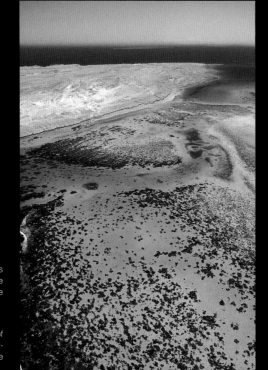

572 and 573
Coral formations and shallow sea floors create almost surreal images in the Strait of Tiran, at the entrance to the Gulf of Aqaba.

574-575
This coral reef lies near the island of Gezira Tawila, which is part of the archipelago between Hurghada and the Sinai Peninsula.

576
The waters of Beacon Rock conceal the wreck of the *Dunraven*, a British merchant ship that hit the coral reef in 1876.

577
A shallow coral sea floor surrounds the island of Qeisum, in the Strait of Gubal between the Sinai Peninsula and the east coast of Egypt.

578
Just a few meters from the shore, the coral reef of Gezr Shâkir, in the Strai of Gubal, drops off suddenly to the sea floor.

579
A small lighthouse signals the dangerous coral reef to ships passing near Hurghada.

580
Divers from around the world are attracted by the unique waters of Shark Reef, near Ras Mohammed.

581
At Ras Mohammed, the coral reef joins the coast, rising at other points to form small off-shore reefs.

582-583
The Ras Mohammed Natural Park forms the southern extremity of the Sinai Peninsula.

584-585
Just past the edge of Ras Mohammed, the Red Sea drops off to a depth of over 2,600 feet 850 meters.)

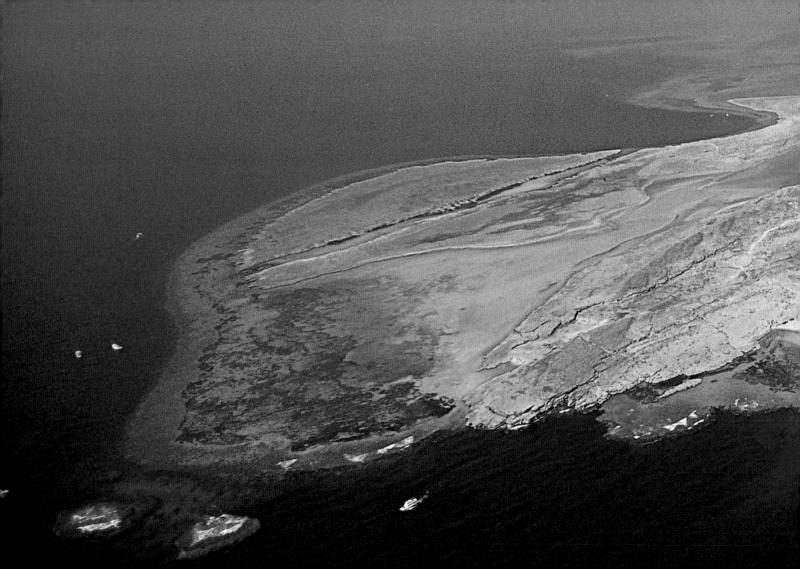

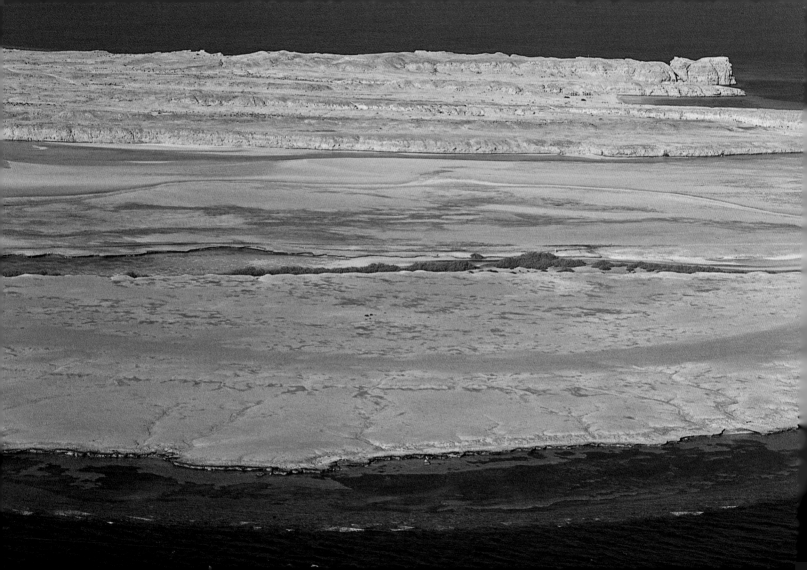

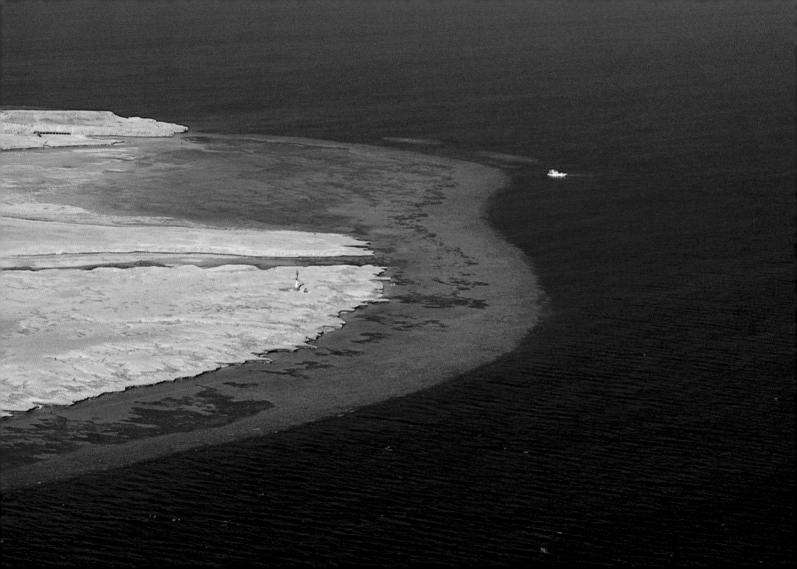

586 and 587
The Ras Mohammed Natural Park was established in 1983 to protect this pristine coastline of the southern Sinai Peninsula.

588-589
The coral reef creates an underwater "step" beneath the irregular coast of Marsa Bereika, inside the Ras Mohammed Natural Park.

590
Shark Observatory, the promontory visible in the foreground, rises to height of about 165 feet (50 meters) next to the Main Beach of Ras Mohammed.

591
Marsa Bareika is the widest inlet along the coast of the Ras Mohammed reserve.

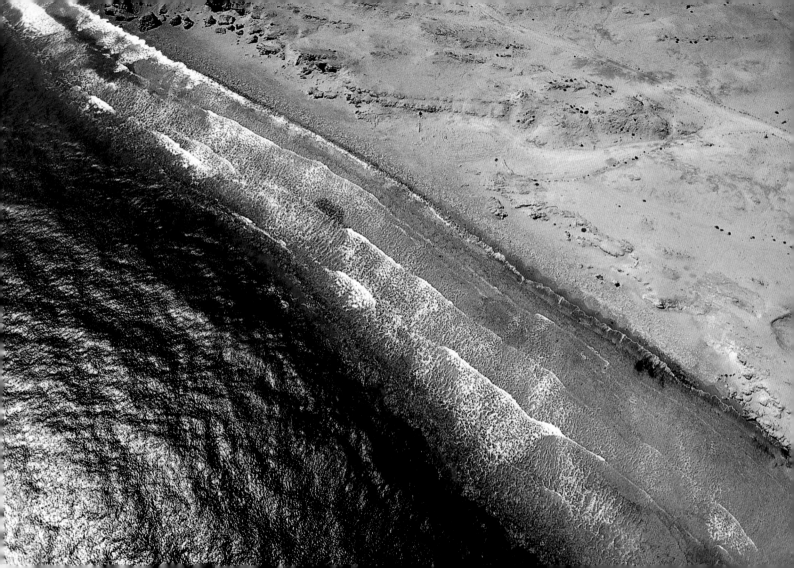

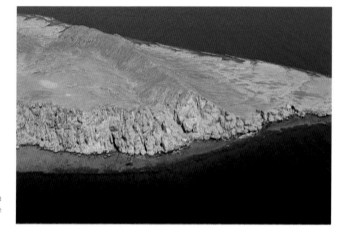

592 and 593
Ras Mohammad originated as a
fossil reef that emerged from the
sea floor 70,000 years ago.

HIGH ABOVE EGYPT

595
The coral reef of the Strait of Tiran offers divers spectacular but demanding dives, due to the powerful currents.

596

A gossamer strip of sand extends into the Gulf of Suez near Ras Gharib, one of the loveliest spots along the Egyptian coast.

597

The coral reef of Gezira Tawila, between the Sinai Peninsula and the east coast of Egypt, creates concentric designs around the island.

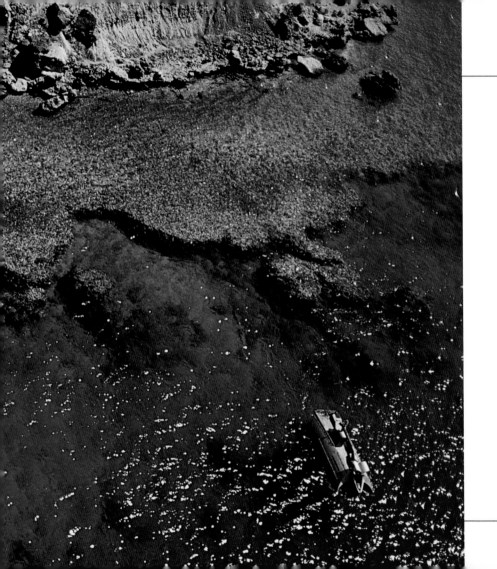

598-599
Numerous private boats transport tourist across the waters near Sharm al-Sheikh to reach the area's unspoiled coastline.

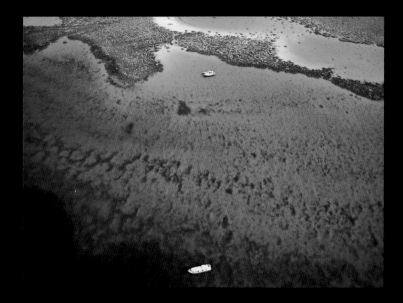

600 and 601
The waters of the Strait of Tiran are so clear that the underwater landscape can easily be seen.

602-603
The coral reef branches out underwater in front of Hurghada, along
the coast of the Red Sea.

604-605
The westernmost end of the island of Sinafir, east of Tiran, is connected to the mainland by a thin isthmus.

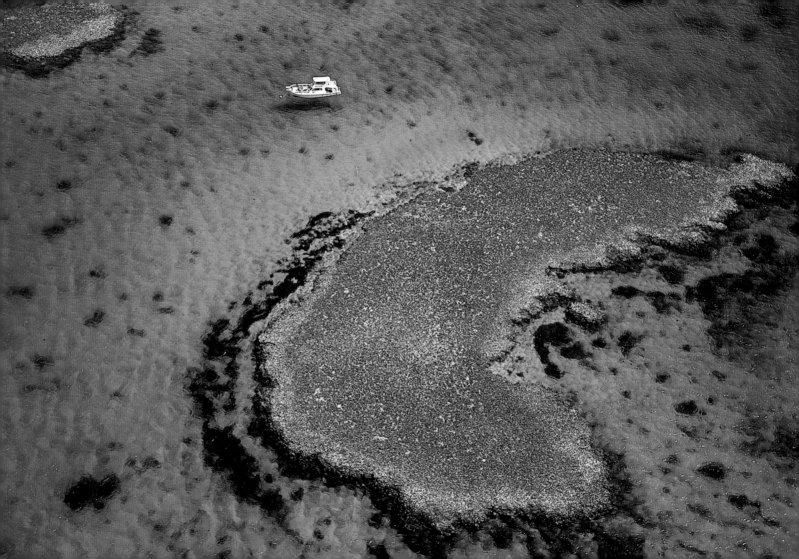

606 and 607
The impressive "sentinel" of the Gulf of Aqaba, the island of Tiran rises in the center of the Strait of Tiran, between the Sinai and Saudi coasts.

608 and 609
The level of the sea forms a sharp break between the bright colors of the coral reefs and the dazzling whiteness of the islands in the Strait of Tiran.

610-611

The coast of Sharm al-Sheikh is not very wide, set between the sea and the tall mountain peaks of the interior of the Sinai Peninsula.

612 and 613
Large hotels, like the Coral Bay Hotel, vie with each other to offer tourists every possible amenity for a seaside vacation, with pools inside the complexes set alongside traditional beaches, and large floating platforms where guests can dive into the sea beyond the coral reef.

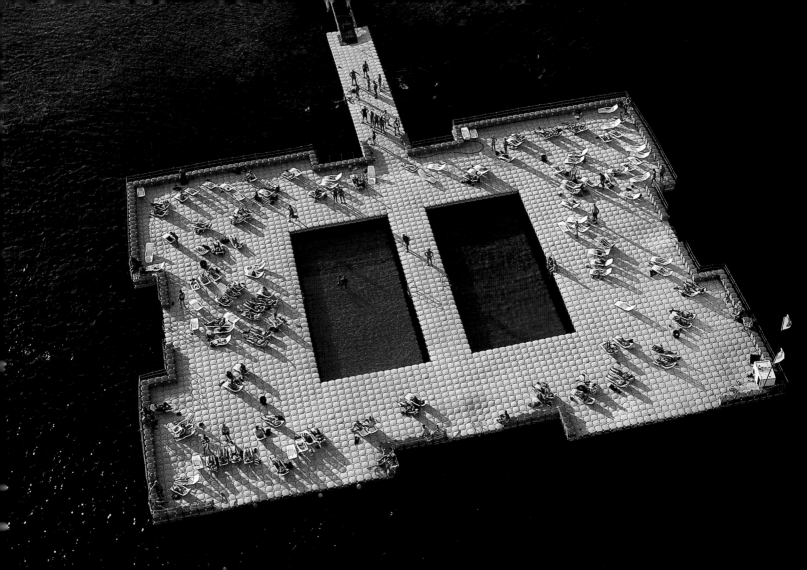

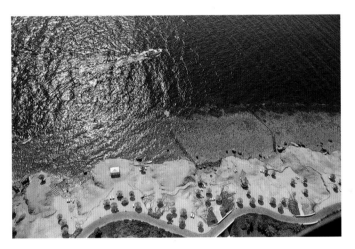

614 and 615
Walkways and landing stages allow visitors to reach deeper water without treading on the corals along the coast of Sharm al-Sheik.

616 and 617
The Nabq nature reserve, north of Sharm al-Sheikh, has a lagoon covered with mangroves reaching towards the sea, where the coral reef is broken up by numerous natural pools.

618 and 619
The mangroves of the Nabq reserve form a narrow but powerful barrier against erosion.

620

Four sections of coral reef extend through the Strait of Tiran. The largest one is Gordon Reef, a popular destination for divers.

621

The wreck of the *Hedoromo Million Hope*, along the coast of the Nabq Nature Reserve, is almost completely submerged-

622-623

The shipwreck trapped on the edge of the Gordon Reef is just one of the many wrecks testifying to the dangers posed by the Red Sea.

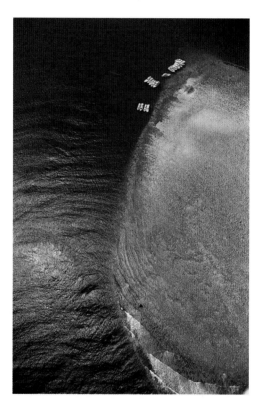

624 and 625
Groups of boats bring swimmers and divers to admire the underwater landscape of the Gordon Reef.

HIGH ABOVE EGYPT

627
The name Dahab, which means "gold" in Arabic, probably comes from the golden yellow color of the sands of the bay.

628-629
Clusters of hard corals and jaggedly outlined areas adorn the underwater landscape of the reef near Sharm al-Sheikh.

630-631
The coasts and all the islands in the area around the southern tip of the Sinai Peninsula are surrounded by the jagged outlines of the coral reef.

632-633
The branch of a coral reef stretches across the Strait of Gubal, south of the Gulf of Suez.

634-635
Contrasts of the Red Sea: brilliant colors and earth tones, florid underwater life, and the emptiness of the desert are just inches (centimeters) apart.

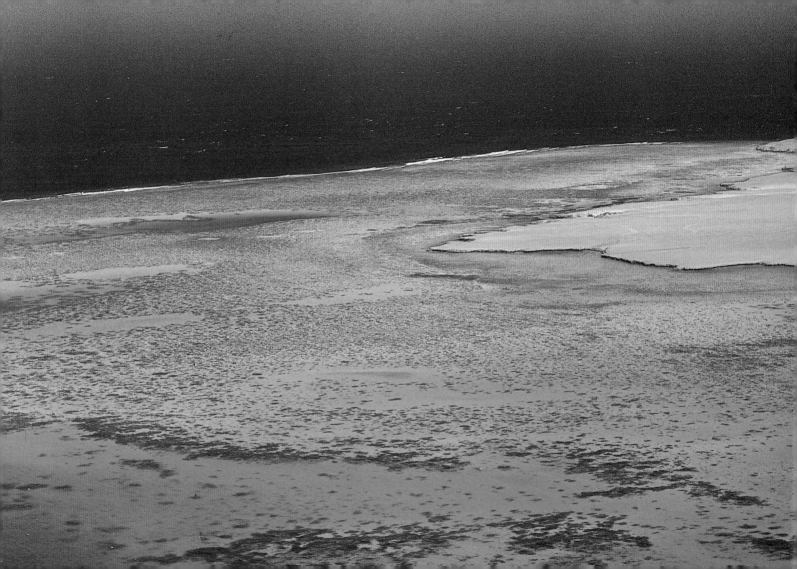

Index

Index

Index

Cover
Deir al-Bahari

Back cover
Siwa Oasis

CORINNA ROSSI GRADUATED FROM THE UNIVERSITY OF NAPLES WITH A DEGREE IN THE HISTORY OF ARCHITECTURE. SHE SUBSEQUENTLY SPECIALIZED IN EGYPTOLOGY, EARNING HER PH.D. AT CAMBRIDGE, WHERE SHE STAYED ON AS JUNIOR RESEARCH FELLOW IN EGYPTOLOGY AT CHURCHILL COLLEGE. SHE CONDUCTS RESEARCH IN THE HISTORY OF ANCIENT ARCHITECTURE AND HAS PUBLISHED NUMEROUS ARTICLES IN SPECIALIZED PERIODICALS. IN 2001, SHE FOUNDED THE NORTH KHARGA OASIS SURVEY, A SURVEY PROJECT OF A CHAIN OF ROMAN FORTRESSES IN EGYPT'S WESTERN DESERT, WHICH SHE CO-DIRECTS.

The publishers would like to thank:
His Excellency Farouk Hosny – Egyptian Minister of Culture; Dr Taha Abd Elaleem – President of the Egyptian Information Center; Apya Shakran – Director General of the Cairo Press Center. A special mention to Gamal Shafik, Cairo Press Center and to Sky Cruise, Cairo, for their cooperation in the balloon photography.

The photograph on page 18 is by Mark Linz.

640

The "natural pyramid" of al-Qurn, the "horn", dominates the Valley of the Kings, still deep in shadow as the first light of dawn arrives.